Poetry Ireland Review 133

Eagarthóir / Editor
COLETTE BRYCE

© Poetry Ireland Ltd 2021

Poetry Ireland CLG/Éigse Éireann CTR gratefully acknowledges the assistance of The Arts Council/An Chomhairle Ealaíon and The Arts Council of Northern Ireland.

LOTTERY FUNDED

Poetry Ireland invites individuals and commercial organisations to become Patrons of Poetry Ireland. For more details, please contact:
Anne Hendrick, Development Manager,
Poetry Ireland, 11 Parnell Square East,
Dublin 1, Ireland
or telephone +353 1 6789815; e-mail development@poetryireland.ie

FOUNDING PARTNERS
Adrian Brinkerhoff Poetry Fund of the Sidney E Frank Foundation
University College Cork

POETRY PATRONS: LYRIC
Joseph Hassett, Marie Heaney, Thomas Dillon Redshaw, Ronan Reid

POETRY PATRONS: SONNET
Marie Baker, Patricia Ferguson, Alan W Gray, Eithne Hand, Neville Keery,
R John McBratney, Joan McBreen, William Pibil, Marian Richardson

POETRY PATRONS: STANZA
Marie Baker, Martina Dalton, Emer Foley, Robert Haughton, Isabel Healy, Monica McInerney, Mary O'Donnell

POETRY PATRONS: HAIKU
Sarah Bannan, Amanda Bell, Peter Clarke, Ciarán Crudden, Kevin Conroy, Karen Hanratty, Christine Dwyer Hickey, Eamon Gillen, Mary Jeffrey, John D Kelly, Susie Kennelly, Karen Meenan, Oliver Mooney, Mike Moran, Jean O'Brien, Eileen O'Donovan, Eilín de Paor, Gillian Perdue, Andy Pollak, John Prebble, Grace Smith, Anne Tannam, Siún Tobin, Patrick Charles Tully, Jesko Zimmerman

Poetry Ireland Review is published three times a year by Poetry Ireland CLG. The Editor enjoys complete autonomy in the choice of material published. The contents of this publication should not be taken to reflect either the views or the policy of the publishers.

ISBN: 978-1-902121-85-7   ISSN: 0332-2998

IRISH-LANGUAGE EDITOR: Aifric Mac Aodha

PUBLICATIONS MANAGER: Paul Lenehan with Eoin Rogers, and with the assistance of Orla Higgins
COVER DESIGN: Alistair Keady (www.hexhibit.com)
COVER CREDIT: *Ice lolly at training*, by Tommie Lehane

Contents

Editorial

As its opening lines will unerringly announce a dull poem, so they do
the surprising and lively one. A common experience of redrafting one's
own poems is the realisation that the first line or lines is not the opening
at all, merely a 'way in' to the subject that can be later dispensed with.
Our best (or more active) opening line may be lying in wait further down
the page. The ability to recognise it and the courage to do away with
our preliminary scene setting is one of the ways in which we improve, if
not as poets then as editors of our own work. Browsing the index of first
lines in a good anthology can be a refreshing reminder of the function
of that opening gambit, to entice the reader to want to read on. Which
poem would you feel compelled to look up, based only on its indexed
line? 'The first line test is a good one', noted the critic Edna Longley; 'has
the poet seized an irresistible momentum from the flux of experience and
language, or is he merely looking out the window, telling you it's a nice
day, and casting around for a subject?' Once in place, a good first line will
exert an extraordinary influence on the form, rhythm, tune, tone, and
subject of the poem; it is fair to say that it determines all that follows.

Beginnings abound in this spring issue. Some debut poets were invited
to reflect on their routes to a first collection. There can be an assumption
these days that poets emerge exclusively through the portals of creative
writing programmes, and this is sometimes an experience related here:
the creation of a peer group and the collective energy generated is high-
lighted as a positive gain. Which reminds me of Flannery O'Connor's
wry remarks: 'Everywhere I go I'm asked if I think the university stifles
writers. My opinion is that they don't stifle enough of them. There's
many a best-seller that could have been prevented by a good teacher.'
Yet, the free-range poet is also always with us, as is the loner, the outlier,
and the late starter. The routes to publication remain as various as the
poetries we write. As Grace Wilentz notes, hearing the stories of others
can be useful as a guide, or spur, in the formation of one's own journey;
it can demystify the sometimes impossible-seeming goal of the first book.

Also in this issue, we listen in on a conversation regarding the Queer
Body in poetry, chaired by Cúirt Festival director Sasha de Buyl. Again,
we have the perspective of relatively new poets, from a generation of
queer writers working in a context of increased acceptance and more
equal rights. Seán Hewitt talks about the moment of risk, in some poems,
when you must 'wrangle with the words or with yourself', the necessity
for courage in the transformative act: 'the more poems you write, the
braver you are'. The transformation of experience into poetry is a process
through which we are often laid open. The poet's vocation has always

required, it seems to me, a coming out, whatever one's identity or how we are positioned in the social world.

Each submission received at *Poetry Ireland Review* is opened with optimism, and I find myself often transfixed by a poem's initial utterance, and then thankfully carried forward by all that follows. One of the sustaining aspects of our art is that it allows us always to begin again, each poem the impossible-seeming thing to be conjured from the swirl of our interior lives; and each followed by a silence into which we hope another poem might, eventually, begin to speak.

– Colette Bryce

Vona Groarke

UNDER A TREE, PARKED

The rain has so much news to impart
it taps on the sunroof and slaps on the glass
and tries its hand at Morse Code, once,
but quickly tires of the subtlety
and shunts to bass-line facts.

This rain seems to be always saying,
"Oh, and another thing",
all its stats and certainties
like shouting in the room where you are
and nowhere else to go.

Jabbing, pinching, full of itself,
this rain insists it be listened to
as if it had the answers, yes,
to every empty question rattling
in this vacant afternoon.

There is no talking back to it.

I am out in the world
and the world is happening
as small stones thrown, repeatedly,
right over my head.

I am tight against it, it would appear;
breathing in what I breathe out
and nothing in between.

Vona Groarke

DAILY NEWS ROUND-UP

For another trick (or the same trick,
played out differently), I will convert rain
to protest and protest to everything,
making rain, into the bargain, a kind of everything.

For this I will need the sound of people
and a cause, a reason to be furious
and right. A start point and an end point
(that is nothing of the sort)

and a street or a park
somewhere with cameras and camera-phones
so the march will be picked up and broadcast
spreading from the west or from the east

depending on which way the wind is blowing
and where you stand, this day.
Then, it's a question of sound effects
of turning the volume up or down:

up, to lose yourself in the noise;
down, to hear yourself think,
as if you lived under galvanized
and the rain has news to shake you up

in how it hits the surface, hard,
so hard you think the roof will cave in
but it doesn't: you're still safe and sound
except back there for a second only

when you thought it fell into your name.

Vona Groarke

FOR NOW

Call it quits on a night of rain,
excitable rain that fizzes and simmers
as though it's been waiting years to declare
what it has to declare, and gives the world
an imperative and an urgency. All we can do
is marshal attention, allow the day to dissolve,
as it does, in the nothing of our doing
and the nothing we have done.

That this rain hammers itself home
barely needs to be said. In between,
in the half-held breath, listen for
a sideways shift from Chains to Change,
Wrong to Rung, Seethe to Seed
and, eventually, No to Now.

Day will happen, will break, they say
and when it's done, they'll say it has broken
and we (by 'we', I mean, of course, You and I)
will spend it fitting edge to edge, hour to hour
to convince ourselves a pattern is discernible
for betterment, for focus, for the best.

Whether we are there to divine it
or whether we are not.

Ella Duffy

RUMOUR

When a worm murmured its word from under the soil,
Rumour took her place, ear to the ground.
The dead arrived as frost; what they had to say
unheard by the living. But Rumour listened,
and with two new tongues spread what she knew
to a town where voices were many,
where someone's daughter, out late,
hand in hand with a girl, was laughing.
The stones heard everything, muttered
along their walls, and a whisper, held in rock,
was quick to tell the sky. The town sent itself to bed
as Rumour's noise reached the sea, always busy
repeating what it knows. Then only salt,
lifting Rumour again, till the birds fed it all back
to the earth, where a worm told another,
told the ruins of a woman, who began to laugh.

Edward Larrissy

LONDON, JUNE 2016

I walked the once-wobbly bridge –
that Blair-years monument –
from Tate to the dome of St. Paul's,
and met the global horde:
the students from Hong Kong
taking selfies which slipped me in,
the schoolkids from Livorno.
A living statue acted
Britannia, a dirty purple,
gleaming a petrol glaze,
with shield and trident staring
towards the wind-whipped river.

Down by the water's edge
the lapping of the waves
on mud and blackened stones
seems louder than the crowds:
a water-clock that quickens
with a passing boat, then slackens
while the gulls bob and stab:
the same as when once traitors
passed in the fated barge
to the watergate at the Tower.

A squall rattles shop-awnings
and rain beats down on traffic
that ceaselessly rips a liquid
plaster from steaming tarmac,
and Union Jacks as big
as blankets flap in a wind
of indecisive moans.
Refugees from the rain
hunch in cathedral darkness,
where confessional whispers echo
in the murmur of distant traffic –
and over the money boxes
the photo of the Blitz
with the dome in a frame of smoke.
But up in the whispering gallery

the walls sweat frightened voices:
'The hordes pour into Albion,
the throne is rocked, our native
liberties extinct.'

A clocktower casts its chimes
across the nervous waters
as if to trumpet forth
the regular construction
of policy and statute:
the chimney of a contraption
that stamps and issues laws
which rise as if through pipes
from an engine room of reflection
and measured dialectic –
and never the place of fevered
lies and mad delusions
where those voices have their spokesmen:
the fish that flitted through
a slippery veil of green;
the fox who ravaged in
the darkened factory farm;
the actor-fop – in fact
a Halifax reborn.

The rain has passed, and now
in dark blue sky with a frame
of clouds, faint stars appear,
and lights come on in flats
and offices by the river.
Raincoats like mayfly wings,
couples walk arm in arm,
or lean against the railings
to photograph the Shard.
Midsummer has just gone,
and soon, with Cancer rising,
darkness will quietly build
like rumours heard in an alley.
So take a final stroll
where the sky seems to widen
with the widening of the river
and promises the world.

Majella Kelly

THE SECRET WIFE OF JESUS

after the painting Fellow Travellers *by Katerina Tsempeli*

It is our first holiday together and the alleyways of Chania see us
holding hands in a way the Latin Quarter of Galway hasn't yet.

Something about a painting draws you, then me, into a gallery.
The couple in it are tourists on a ferry, unaware of the artist's gaze.

The man's elbow rests on a railing, his right hand surrendered
to the woman, who stands over it, focused as a manicurist.

We see him watching her from under a piece of white muslin, cast
loosely over him. His dark beard makes the scene feel biblical,

but also, ever-so-slightly erotic, as our eyes follow the trailing
strings of a polka-dot bikini down the curve of her spine to a low-

slung sarong. We wonder what it is she could be doing ... maybe
removing a thorn or something? Behind them, sea and sky merge

in blue and purple hues that bleed into their outlines, to halo them
in a greenish light so divine, it looks like the wedding of Helios

and Artemis, where the moon is holding the outstretched hand
of the sun. We move closer, to see how the artist has done it.

Fine lines in the acrylic and oil pastels are like the secrets of a lost
gospel where Mary Magdalene was never a prostitute

and where the Son of God was conceived during a night of mind-
blowing sex. You are thinking of the word *forgiveness*, for some reason.

I reach for another: *worship*. The artist's husband, Kostas, offers us
a shot of raki and limoncello. Our tongues warm with aniseed

and citrus. We wander into a church after that. There is mass on.
A handful of people are filing up to communion. I get the sudden urge

to receive, though it's forbidden, and for you too, us being divorced
and, clearly unrepentant about it, therefore: sinners.

Squeezing hands and smiling, we make for the bright light of the exit.
I conjure up the couple from our Aegean terrace later. They drink

wine and break bread into sweet Cretan olive oil. I close my eyes.
Then Jesus, to the bridal chamber, he leads me with torches.

Majella Kelly

FIG

No wonder it wasn't familiar
to you, this love, the way it planted itself
as the fig tree did against the brick wall
of the old lean-to glass house whose roof
was shattered by winter storms. And readily
it grew in the average loam, leaves fragrant
and deeply lobed. But a fig is not a fruit,
it's a flower and, like a fig, this love bloomed
inward. You didn't love me, you said,
but I waited. A fig will never ripen
in a bowl. You must know the exact time
to pick it. Touch it, skin to skin, to feel
the exquisite velvet bloom. Squeeze it gently
from its base to see it weep a perfect tear.

The glass house's skeletal frame struggles
to stay upright. This love is ripe now, my love,
split it, taste the complex inflorescence,
love's core of tiny edible blossoms.
How seemingly seedless it is, but all
the more luscious for it. What is love anyway
but an abundance of figs underfoot
in the midday sun, browsed upon by wasps.

Mícheál McCann

IMMANENCE

A raspberry one with moist frosting, or
a lemon one with white chocolate shavings?
A door chime signals us. A donut for two in
a café with notions on a sleepy Lisburn Road.
The low buzz chat of other people engaged
in another try. Exposed soft white light bulbs
make everything rounder. Do you see them?
Some good coffee. Two brightly green eyes.

Hammers of wet coffee grounds into the bin
remind us we're here; our treasure is delivered.
What we have been waiting for all this time.
Slowly, a dull blade halves the red-glaze donut
and it cries laughing. Blood is coming out!
You're wearing my jumper. You're eating.

Mícheál McCann

BIG CITY TYPES

Now we'll certainly be stopping
cultchie-this and *plaid-shirt-shone-*
brown-shoes-that, indeed; and less
of your lamenting us poor folks'
long days under wakening
and path-clearing rains.
Don't you worry heavy-bagged traveller,
we'll manage. And let's agree
to never again recall your idea
that those who stay here in this city,
run through by a windingly grey and bracing river,
are engaged in a constant political act.

Where we live our days is as varied as wildflower,
blooming steadily or shifting colour and place.
Don't feel bad for those
who are not seduced by heat or change,
they have their own blessed concerns.
Anchors are only found in the sea.
Come along now, a plane is planning
to take you away from here,
and the rain will still fall, and the days persist
varied and expansive as an orrery,
or the shadows of people on often
rebuilt, well-walked walls.

Keep chasing the sun long enough
and you'll meet your shadow coming back.

Kimberly Reyes

STAIN IN CREASES

> *"The whole answer is there on the canvas."*
> – Edward Hopper

A walk through the
Gallery, a history

Walker and Weems see
Too much

Interned wings,
Loud, counter migration

To which I then need,
Prefer, the art of echo

That may be realism (?)
A cosy invisibility –

Picture me bussing
In 'Chop Suey'

Would I have been
In the kitchen, at Phillies?

In the pantry storing
Watching, growing

The darker brother ...
I, too, am America

Ars Americana
An etching of desolation

I can never put into
A proper word

And I don't know
But need to think how

He'd see straight through
Me, if we ever didn't meet

Kerry Hardie

INSOMNIA IN TALBOT STREET

The Americans who woke me
with goodnights in the corridor at 4 a.m.
have drowned in their pillows.

Now, lying, the streetlight spread on the wall,
the lace at the window
laid on the light on the wall,

its scallops and figures
fashioned in shadow, the immaculate draft
of each fold.

*

The anger that I carry
against the morning, its too-soon coming,
is toiled in me like Flemish lace,

is rich and wrought
as Flemish lace
that ruffled throats and wrists and breasts,

that complicated
and augmented
the body's daily journey through the halls.

*

It seems there is to be
no drift-away,
not even a small loosening

as the walls grey,
as sounds thicken
and burst their stretched skins.

Day presses at the window,
urgent, close.
Styled and dressed to go in nylon net.

Damian Smyth

KEATS'S BED
23.02.1821

After death, control precautions count. The police have been.
Furniture, floor, even the walls, everything to be destroyed
By order of the law, as if the infection's on the iron bedframe,
Fireplace, antimacassar; as perhaps it is.
                                    Dr C is looking to all that.
A death by strangulation, suffocation, drowning; and all
From that 'fawn-coloured mixture' of phlegm and blood,
Spat out a year before, now 'black and thick in the extreme',
Coming up in cupfuls. The body, opened like a wardrobe,
Shows lungs on hangers inside, his shirts already burned.
                               It hasn't rained for three months,
Not properly. The moonshot has failed in Florida, but there's
Still a living to be made, watching the skies; now we know
Once more he has just this minute gone, his room cleared,
The lost upholstery of coughing, microscopic, and everywhere.

Tamara Barnett-Herrin

SOFT PLAY

When my mother asked me
whether the nursery teacher had done more
than rub my back to soothe me at naptime,
we were both a bit drunk.
I did that *Umm, rilly?* thing,
and she said *Bad man!* as if to attack him.
But were he to have hurt me then,
now would be too late.

I worried this all night, and asked her to explain,
the next day. We were at soft play.
There was a sound of ever-present screaming
as all around us breathless children raced and climbed,
threw things and slid. A plastic scaffolding cube
of many levels and depths,
containing swings and pits and bridges and drops
was built inside a barn where cows once calved.
Now, there was a blue sky painted on the ceiling,
and a beaming sun.

What did you mean? I asked her.
Did you know something – something terrible?
No, no, she said. It was just resurgent guilt
over leaving me in another's care.
No ugly photograph exists,
presumably, of me aged 3, being abused.
It was her shame at letting me go
that troubled her still, and made me feel so unsafe,
even now, in this weird barn.

I stood up and looked at the structure,
within which my daughters squirmed somewhere.
It was like a ticking hive. Very many children, very
busy, like maggots, cleaning off putrescence
from an amputation. I saw them explode from a chute,
then lost, then found them, again and again,
my eye tracing their trails,
like a finger that feels every curlicue
of an ironwork barrier,
or circles the crenelated edges of a graze.

Outside the rain fell on polytunnels of strawberries
and hunched birds of prey,
hooded and tethered in the dripping falconry.
The screaming volume lessened
when I had the girls close to me. The more
I looked into their eyes, the quieter it got.
A thought had grabbed me,
and as we wrestled,
outside the ring that bordered my fear,
all my other thoughts roared and cheered.

Tamara Barnett-Herrin

HI! IS THIS FOR ME?

for CR

Everything's open,
she wrote,
and sent
by accident.

Hi!
Is this for me?
I replied,
by text.

When these happenings
occur, they pull us
very close
together.

This stray intimacy
is an essential
property of being.

As is the way
that everything
is open
to meaning.

To sending,
and to receiving.

Thomas McCarthy

A MEADOW IN JULY

It's just that a poem is forming a meadow
For itself. And then a window –
Not a modern window at all but an old, flaking
Casement thing, ropes and pulleys

And weights you could hear
Banging inside their unpainted timber frames.
The deepest thing has a rumble
That you can never see,

A distant thunder in a thundery July;
The way poems heave in their nervousness
Before small birds hit the windows,
Thinking poetry is a drift of insects

Or some such promise of food.
We gaze beyond our rooms in idleness,
Idly dreaming of things outside ourselves,
A full plate that we intuit

Before we come to our senses
In that hide-out the poem has made
Between our faces and July. See, it's the same poem
Has placed glass between us and a meadow.

Bernard O'Donoghue

L'AIUOLA

> 'L'aiuola che ci fa tanto feroci'
> – *Paradiso* 22.151

In the morning it was raining, so
we were sent unwillingly to school.
But when it dried up before midday
the thresher made its lumbering way along
the road past the playground, pale pink top-boards
a slow glimpse through the blackthorn hedges.
Was it coming to us? A miracle:
our father's hat framed in the dim glass
of the classroom half-door, motioning to us.
He'd left the busy threshing floor behind
to drive the mile to school to bring us home
for the most celebrated feast day of the year.

Likewise, when Theresa died in hospital
my mother had to go to break the news.
"Theresa is not good, Jula." "Must we go to Cork?"
"She's worse than that, Jula." So they drove to school
to bring her sister and her brothers home.
But it was not a busy scene of threshing
they brought them to, but the flower-garden
that Theresa had tended all her short life.

Bernard O'Donoghue

THE IMPULSATOR

It was rare for people other than family
To stay overnight with us: two Poor Clares
From Manchester on one occasion;
A White Father with a bulbous scooter
Who'd met our cousin out on the Missions;
Two lady teachers from Shakespeare's Stratford
Who didn't stay in the house, but puzzlingly
Slept in their campervan on the grass outside.

But when the Simplex milking-machine went wrong
A man called Joyce from Galway came to check
The Impulsator which always seemed
To be the trouble. On the Sunday morning
My mother knocked on his bedroom door
And asked if he wanted to get up for Mass,
But he said that he was 'Church of Ireland',
And turned his back, observing his persuasion.

Siobhán Campbell

THE OUTHOUSE

Whitewashed when they held stations in the house
though none would visit here, the outhouse.
Crusted and greening where the wall meets the gravel,
stained under the eaves where a creamy fungus grows.
The door opens as if something stops it from behind.
Inside is a reverence of air as if quiet has lain here in wait.
A bucket in the corner, two spades, a *sleán* for footing turf.
On one wall, a Sunday suit, black with a narrow stripe,
the one he wore when they committed the aunt, never
to come out again, all land forfeited. His crutches
hang here too, as if displayed, side by side, an exhibit
of what not to do, ready for him if ever he returned
still limping, still with the gangrened toe but with his
own head in tatters, his mind three sheets to the wind.

Tim McGabhann

MORELIA GHOSTS

i

Red-eyed, wasted, grief-winded,
driving away from the funeral,
my face in the jeep's windscreen
was a dazed, sad child's.

Every sip of hip-flask vodka
made steppe-grasses stoop
and brush my palate.

I pulled into Morelia
way past the hour of anything good,
stopped at a hotel whose gable end

was lost to a rain-mizzle
that darkened the cobbles
and lacquered them with muck.

Under the eaves,
a lamp-swinging phantom
who'd nipped in for shelter
to rub his skinny arms.

Inside, I drew the curtains,
cabled up for the plunge,
every vein baby-loud and greedy
for poppy-scud, spore-scatter,
that goneness warmer
than the bosom of Abraham.

ii

The TV showed a late film, some army kid
from a town of smoky-eaved apothecaries,

the art in him pressed out by military school,
when he wished his life would flow like water.

The logo for the TV brand was the Greek god Mercury,
a blotched silver mascot, one finger to his lips.

A sea's shallow vowels played on repeat
and futzed the TV's speakers with little rushes of static.

A mother and son golf on a cliff, whack out
little bone comets that briefly whiten the night.

That sea's where I'd most like to ebb,
clouds coming apart overhead like brains sent spinning,

the shredded brass of lit rain, the red
plane-warning lights at the power-plant

blinking me on and off.

   iii

Now a scorpion naps
under the bathroom sink

where little knots of blood
have been fraying up through the water.

A cricket scritches
his little violin

from a shelf above the desk.
Outside, shin-deep in fog,

jornaleros yawn, groan,
kick pebbles

and wait for the jeeps
to bring them to the ranches

where the picking pays double
but sometimes costs everything.

iv

Skite up the pipe, little spectre,
shard the terracotta tiles,

throw down the flashing
until the pickups turn around

give these men
just one empty day –

and, while you're at it,
because what prayer is full

unless it holds the one praying it,
pick me up in your eely fingers

and drop me into the heart's lake-muck,
and let my head nod, a weed underwater,

the tide-pulse's amniotic rocking
a thrum in me from boss of skull

to the fat of each toe.

v

Then bright trolley-tattle
steam, a bucket of tamales
propped on the child-seat

beside a long tusk
of styrofoam cups
and a jar of claggy Nescafé –

a mother-and-daughter team
their giggles a kite
straggling up

in brilliant flags.

Grace Wilentz

WORKING TOWARDS THE LIMIT OF LIGHT

Resolve

The process of working towards my first full collection started in earnest in late 2015. Though I had been writing for more than a decade, a series of big changes, including getting my Irish citizenship, meant that I suddenly felt myself on enough solid ground to pursue the dreams I'd put on hold during years of being in 'survival mode'. Though a book felt very far away, I wanted to begin publishing again and become part of the poetry community in Ireland. I signed up for a workshop, and convinced some of my classmates to keep meeting as a monthly writers' group. By 2016, I was publishing my first poems in Ireland. *Skylight 47*, *Poetry Ireland Review*, and *Cyphers* were among the first to accept my work. After having three poems appear in *The Irish Times*, I was approached by two publishers interested in seeing a full manuscript. I felt delighted and also terrified – I knew I wasn't ready to publish a collection. So, I sent a sample and did my best to keep the conversation going.

Slowing down

Over a year I'd written 20-40 poems I was pretty happy with, and I started keeping them in a soft binder, experimenting with changing the order, and thinking about what the gaps were in terms of the tone and a coherent narrative. But the more I worked on the manuscript, the smaller it became. I was also working full time on the Repeal campaign, and though that was a once-in-a-lifetime opportunity, it was full on. I started to feel guilty about letting the chance to be published slip away. Out of a desire to work on something smaller before the bigger project of a full collection, I submitted to Green Bottle Press's pamphlet competition, and was selected. It was a positive experience and an opportunity to deal with things like contracts, covers, launches, and all the details a poet has to face for the first time. After that, things came into sharper focus. I applied for an Arts Council grant, and unlike all the other times when I asked for a fraction of the grant amount, unsuccessfully, I asked for the full whack and pitched a plan to devote a significant portion of my year to finish my collection. This time, I got it.

Finding silence

The Arts Council literature bursary changed my life. I wasn't eking out a poem while riding the bus, or last thing before bed. I could wake up fresh, make coffee, and make my way to the desk. It gave me a glimpse into how I want to live. It afforded me time to read many first collections and get a sense of their 'shape'. It allowed me to take up a month-long residency in a little fishing village in Iceland where there was a supermarket and a petrol station, and that was it. No café, no pub, no distractions. It delivered silence, incredible sunsets, wild horses, and, of course, the Northern Lights. I did a full edit of the manuscript and wrote a significant amount of new work.

A trusted reader

After the residency, I was focused on completing the book. As I worked, it became clear what belonged and what didn't. The manuscript was separating, and I allowed myself to cut a lot of work. I came to see which were the 'pillar' poems around which the manuscript was built. I also worked on some poems that I saw as setting up the next book I want to write. For about four months, I worked on the collection as a whole every morning. Though I had a sense of the trajectory of it, I printed everything out and arranged it on the floor, making adjustments as I walked through it. I thought long and hard about the risks I was taking, and consciously took them anyway. I found joy in the process, and I hope that comes through in the work. I only showed the manuscript to one person I really trust, my friend Alexander Rothman. Letting someone into the manuscript is a pretty vulnerable place. He read it with such care, gave me his reading of each poem, reflected on the structure, and suggested dividing the poems into four sections. His support meant the world to me, and gave me the confidence I needed to know it was time. I made adjustments and sent it to a professional proofreader. I set a date for myself by which the manuscript would go, and unlike most things in my life, did not let myself be rushed or late. I chose a date that is an auspicious feast day in my tradition – it couldn't hurt, right?

Letting go

I was very lucky to work with an editor who treated the work with respect. Edits were light, but strengthening. Working with the team at The Gallery Press, I knew my book was in safe hands. *The Limit of Light* launched in October 2020. Putting something out into the world that comes from your heart is always revealing. No one told me how weird it would feel until the night of my pamphlet launch, and I was grateful for the tip as it helped me to understand my mixed emotions. Now I know to prepare myself, and to take lots of time and space for self-care after publication. Of course there is joy, too, especially in the people who you've never met who seek you out with their thanks, praise, invitations, and reflections. Of all the things I have done in my life, I think it's publishing my first collection that I am most proud of, because of having the courage to do it, and for realising a long-held dream. On my own journey, I wished very much for someone to act as a guide, and I hope this glimpse into my process helps to support other poets make their own way.

Katie Donovan

DIGNITY, DEFIANCE, RECLAMATION

Matthew Sweeney, *Shadow of the Owl* (Bloodaxe Books, 2020), £10.99.
Michael Gorman, *Fifty Poems* (Artisan House, 2019), €18 hb.
Geraldine Mills, *Bone Road* (Arlen House, 2019), €15.

Dignity in the face of human vulnerability is a shared thread in these new collections by Matthew Sweeney, Michael Gorman, and Geraldine Mills. Bristling with defiance and absurdist humour, Sweeney's *Shadow of the Owl* is the last collection he wrote before his death from Motor Neurone Disease in 2018. Michael Gorman's *Fifty Poems* embraces the lives of the marginalised in small-town Ireland. Including photographs and documents, Geraldine Mills's *Bone Road* is a searing excavation of the emigrant story of her maternal grandmother's family. I want first to disclose that my poetry is also published by Bloodaxe Books. Ireland being small, and the poetry scene even more so, such overlaps are inevitable.

Readers will be familiar with Sweeney's frequent inclusion of the grotesqueries of death in the 'alternate reality' his work usually inhabits. The poems in *Shadow of the Owl* tackle the actual reality of his impending death with undiminished eccentricity and insight. In language by turns satiric and heart-rending, Sweeney charts the arrival of his diagnosis and the slow deterioration of his body. Reminiscent of Ciaran Carson's magnificent *Still Life*, also written in the last, terrible phase of a terminal disease, this collection shows Sweeney marshalling his distinctive poetic gifts.

The tone is loose and chatty, with details of espressos quaffed and jazz as a soundtrack. However, in poems such as the superb 'Crucifixion', Sweeney's craft underpins each line:

> The first man grinned, shaking his bag of nails
> and patting the hammer in his belt. 'We've come
> to carry out your crucifixion.' Seeing my reaction
> he laughed, 'Don't worry it's all been paid for.'

The poet's solitary struggle metamorphoses into scene after scene of nightmarish role-play. In the twelve-part opening sequence, 'The Owl', he is tortured by a cruelly elusive owl who will not tell him what is happening. As the poems unspool, we are introduced to other bizarre threats, including the Sirens, a hungry crocodile, a sadistic portrait painter, a three-headed monster, and a hangman with gallows. The poet must use his wits to escape – often navigating Cork City's 'Shakey Bridge', which adds to the sense of precarious danger in these noir-ish fables: 'I keep waiting for a blast of gunfire – / I know their type, if they can't find / me they'll shoot someone else' ('Butterflies').

Cheery details of outfits donned, boiled eggs consumed, and the unpredictable state of his bowels bring this nervy, witty personality vividly to life, even as the disease exacts its toll: 'They claim I could even still eat, with the tube / sticking out of me, but how could I revel in / a *Wiener Schnitzel* with that encumbrance? ... I want to be myself till the last minute' ('The Tube'). A poet of uncompromising gifts, Sweeney's demise is a blow to the world of Irish poetry, which has lost too many of its major voices in recent years.

Michael Gorman's *Fifty Poems* is a handsomely produced hardback. Colourful artwork by Joe Boske complements Gorman's penchant for the surreal. Gorman has had a prolonged period of silence since his last collection, *Up She Flew*, was published by Salmon in 1991, and *Fifty Poems* includes earlier work along with new poems. Like Sweeney and Mills, he relishes intimate human details such as clothes, physical ailments, place-names, and food.

In spite of its nondescript title, *Fifty Poems* buzzes with stories. Many are about Gorman's boyhood in Sligo, combining nostalgia with an awareness of hardship and hypocrisy. Yeats is mentioned in a mocking context in 'The Power of Verse', and Gorman echoes one of Yeats's best-known quotes in 'Companions': 'Show me your friends, my boy, / and I'll tell you who you are.'

In stripped back, unsentimental language, he highlights small, local details to portray 'lost causes': 'Benny Kirwan, pale, bald, / Protestant shop-assistant in Lydon's Drapery. / One Wednesday, the town's half-day, / he hanged himself from a tree / on the shore at Lough Gill' ('The People I Grew Up With Were Afraid'). He holds a mirror up to timid lives:

> And what were they afraid of? Rent
> collectors, rate collectors, insurance men.
> Things to do with money. But,
> especially of their vengeful God.

In darkly hilarious poems such as 'Cresting the Wave' and 'Love Is for Life', stuffed with ironic drama and droll dialogue, Gorman shows himself to have much in common with the multi-talented Dermot Healy: 'When Dervla mentions the word 'mucus' / in an entirely sexual context, / the spiritual advisor, Fr. O'Carroll, / quietly leaves the room.'

Gorman finds his inspiration in forgotten landscapes and simple, significant gestures, whether it is the memory of the feel of his sister's hand in his on the way home from school, or the daily rounds of an eccentric flâneur. The effect is both poignant and unsettling: 'he'd cross to Grattan Street and the Grosvenor Guest / House, closed for years but still displaying a TRY OUR DELICIOUS / ICES sign in the window above a drawing of two English / children, a boy and a girl, eating cones of a type never available / in Sligo' (from the prose poem 'Joachim').

Many Irish families have been fragmented by forced emigration due to poverty. In 1883, Geraldine Mills's maternal great-grandparents, Philip and Mary Heveron, along with their six children, left Doolough in Co. Mayo for a new life in America. With support from the Quaker Tuke Fund, they settled in Warren, Rhode Island, where Philip found work in the local mill. After only eighteen months, they decided to return to Ireland – once again facing hardship, and the death of one of their daughters in a Cork workhouse.

This family history forms the background to *Bone Road*. Mills's intent – to dignify her ancestors by reclaiming the trials of their journeying – gives her collection some similarity to documentary poetry (for more on this, see Ailbhe Darcy's fascinating essay 'Recent Documentary Poetry in Performance' in the last issue of *Poetry Ireland Review*, 132).

However, it is Mills's lyric poetry, honed with delicacy and restraint, which haunts the reader long after we have ceased looking at the photographs and documents which serve merely as parallel illustration. In 'Witness', she gives a moving account of the Famine scenes which were the motivation for the establishment of the Tuke Fund:

> a place where the poor sucked stones
> from the road, ate their children's hair,
> were blown like chaff
> into the lake's unsated mouth

Using the potent symbol of the heated coin to create a peep-hole onto the affluent streets of Warren, Mills shares what the newly transplanted Mary imagines as she looks out the window: 'She sees herself in a landau, / with its Moroccan leather and broadlace.' Philip Heveron is furious at his daughter's costly fantasies: 'his rimed breath freezes their waking dream, / turns it icy white.'

The drive to return to Ireland seems to have been mostly Philip's, and is rendered in all its complexity in poems such as 'He Longs for Bog Cotton'. As for Mills's grandmother Brigid, she survives the workhouse to finally achieve the life of plenty her sister Mary once dreamed of – not in America but at home in Ireland: 'Lace cuffs at her wrists / the fur collar of her coat / warming the pearls at her neck [...] the last traces of the pauper / have been cleaved from her.'

Mills's poetry is a stark reminder of the bigotry of imperialism. 'The Missing Link' describes a British 'head measuring' expedition to the West of Ireland in the 1890s, in order to prove 'the natives' nigrescence'. Another poem, 'By Design', highlights the brutal attitude of the Poor Law Commissioner entrusted to oversee the construction of a workhouse: 'How can we control their numbers if fever / isn't let race through these structured flues / like wonder flows through summer?'

The fate of the First Nations tribes who welcomed the Europeans into their territory is not ignored: 'When the new settlers landed at Sowams [...] They wiped its true name from their lips. / Called it their own; / the one James Tuke knew it by / and centuries later sent my people to' ('What the New Settlers Saw'). A personal history with a far reach and a fine sense of craft, this is a collection that will resonate with many.

Against a background of bitterness, hunger, and regret, these new collections by Sweeney, Gorman, and Mills offer a vision of human endurance. With humour, vivid detail, and the grace of understatement, each in its own fashion achieves a powerful effect.

Hugh Haughton

EXIT MAHON, STAGE LEFT: *WASHING UP*

'I shall die in due course on a day of rain', Mahon anticipates in his last book, while stipulating 'Not in the last bed by the exit please, / with a loud sitcom on the gogglebox / but in an armchair at the twilight hour / reading something favoured by old crocks: / gossip, philosophy, maybe Schopenhauer'. Commemorating Yeats, Auden said that 'The death of the poet was kept from his poems.' 2020, however, was a year in which the deaths of three of Ireland's most important poets coincided with the publication of a final collection, making it hard to keep their deaths and poems apart. Fortunately, Derek Mahon left the stage of Irish poetry with the same panache with which he arrived in 1968 with *Night-Crossing*, leaving us a formally elegant, intellectually flamboyant, and fiercely contrarian final collection under the beautifully unlikely title of *Washing Up*. It brings together gossip, philosophy, and evidence of much reading, espousing both the chattiness of 'old crocks' and the 'gogglebox', and the mischievous and musical pleasures of rhyme (like 'twilight hour' with 'Schopenhauer'). Mahon took his final bow after Ciaran Carson (who died in 2019) and Eavan Boland, two other poets who changed the Irish poetic constitution, and Mahon's 'A True Note' pays fitting tribute to Carson's 'skipping, fluent song' and 'nimble tongue'. In another new poem, Mahon says 'Now, watching friends begin their afterlives, / contemporaries around me fall like leaves, / I fear for the future relevance of the art', aligning himself with poets of the past who 'would write / out of conviction and tormented insight / into the workings of the world.' *Washing Up* lines up behind Boland's *The Historians* and Carson's *Still Life* as testament to a long, many-minded, and influential career, driven by his own 'tormented insight' into the 'workings of the world'. Its final poem, 'Word to the Wise', is dedicated to the poet-president – 'A Uachtaráin' – Michael D Higgins, and praises his resistance to 'ecocide', his devotion to 'a more equitable, radical, / *heartening* socio-economic model', and finally his 'panache and fortitude'.

Those words, 'panache' and 'fortitude', apply to Mahon himself, who showed admirable intellectual courage and technical resilience in confronting the crisis, waste, and damage in the world around him and in himself (he is a great poet of damage). He showed an equally intransigent commitment to what Wallace Stevens calls 'the gaiety of language', the sheer force of the aesthetic. The combination of panache and crisis is visible as early as 'Rage for Order' (set against the 'Burnt-out / buses' of his native Belfast), and again in 'Courtyards in Delft', where he imagines himself as 'A strange child with a taste for verse', confronted by the 'esurient sea' and 'hard-nosed companions' with their 'dream of war'.

The same sense of bruised survival and stylistic panache is in play in 'After the Titanic' and 'Ovid in Tomis', as well as such heart-breaking autobiographical lyrics as 'Craigvara House' (where we are told 'home is where the heart breaks') and 'Dawn at St Patrick's', where the poet, recovering in a psychiatric hospital, talks of being a 'make-believe existentialist' in his 'Protestant bed'. A comparable dialectic is played out in the two experimental sequences of the 1990s, particularly *The Hudson Letter* (now *New York Time*). An account of his own alcoholic breakdown and recovery, the collage-like poem also offers a hallucinatory documentation of crisis in Manhattan, rewriting *The Waste Land* in the neo-liberal USA in the wake of Lowell, Plath, and Berryman, and haunted by down-and-outs, psychos, and the ghosts of Hart Crane, Elizabeth Bishop, Auden, and a host of others, who also made art out of 'tormented insight'. Formally and thematically, such poems capture the chaotic complexity and violence of late capitalist postmodernity, as well as the damaged poet's rage for order and renewal.

In the title poem of the new book, Mahon describes himself as a 'widower' washing up under a 'bright star' at the kitchen sink, and as:

> a relic of pre-digital times,
> fond of anachronistic rhymes,
> in flight from the new *politique*
> of induced squalor and high tech
> washed up on a deserted beach
> grumpy, contrarian, out of reach.

The self-portrait of the poet as a 'strange child with a taste for verse' from 'Courtyards in Delft' may have morphed into 'grumpy, contrarian', 'washed up on a deserted beach', but the Audenesque panache and acerbic Swiftian rhymes insist on the battle as well as the bond between the 'new *politique*' and his insouciant aesthetic. Matthew Campbell has written memorably about 'The Irish Longing for Rhyme', and Mahon's continually re-inventive commitment to 'anachronistic rhymes' is a crucial ingredient in the fierce and genial late style of *Washing Up*.

In 'A Visitor from Rio de Janeiro', Paul Durcan recounts walking along Sandymount Strand, that primal scene of Irish literature, and bumping into 'a sea-faring man – / In an off-white mac / Sauntering past us'. This results in a breezy recognition scene:

> It is the poet Mahon.
> Captain of my nation
> Revolving in the sharpish breeze –
> Sharpish for June –
> He smiles that Dublin Bay smile of his.

Durcan imagines the Brazilian visitor's weekend as 'Epitomized by the poet Mahon', as Mahon 'bows out' and the two of them 'walk on / Talking about him in front of his back. / Literally – just as he would wish it.' Durcan defines fame as 'having all Ireland / Talking about you / In front of your back.'

Now Mahon has finally bowed out, Durcan's comic vignette acquires a different tonality. My hunch is that all Ireland will continue talking about him after his typically stylish exit. Though latterly Mahon exchanged that Dublin Bay for Kinsale Harbour, he retained the nautical air of a well-travelled dandy, sporting a combination of jacket, cravat, and sneakers. He still has a claim to be a kind of alternative national 'captain', less magisterial and professorial than Heaney and Boland, say, but with comparable authority. Marianne Moore talked of the poet as a 'literalist of the imagination', and Mahon is not only such a literalist – writing a poetry that thrives on concrete detail, specific light effects, and named places – but our greatest littoralist of the imagination. From the early 'Day Trip to Donegal' to 'Washing Up', where he goes to 'watch the sea / washing up in the estuary', he is never happier than haunting the coast (many of his best lines are coast lines). Translating Valéry's 'Le cimetière marin' brilliantly as 'The Seaside Cemetery', Mahon's oeuvre includes an astonishing series of poems about the Irish coast. To list some of his titles is to take a tour from the Northern Ireland of 'North Wind: Portrush', 'The Sea in Winter', 'Rathlin', 'Cushendun in Winter', and 'A Bangor Requiem'; travelling southwards to 'Beyond Howth Head' and 'A Swim in Co. Wicklow'; and on to the West Cork of 'Harbour Lights', 'Bashō in Kinsale'; and round to the West Coast in 'Aran', and 'The Mayo Tao'.

But though we mourn the death of a naturalist of a new ecological kind in the later Mahon – he is the author of a 'Homage to Gaia' as well as 'Homage to Goa' – he was also a poet of culture, or rather cultures, and the first of a new kind of transnational city poet in Irish poetic history. The first poem of New Collected Poems, 'Spring in Belfast', conjures the 'echoing back streets of this desperate city'. The cultural fascination of the modern metropolis is integral to Mahon's vision. Take the light that 'streaks the walls / Of Georgian houses, pubs, cathedrals' of Dublin in 'Beyond Howth Head', or London, 'Rain-fresh in morning light' in 'Afterlives', or the 'clutch of gantries ... skirts and shirts mid-20th century style / in dimly lit arcades' recalled in 'Brian Moore's Belfast'. This last poem (a counterpart of 'Camus in Ulster') is a reminder that Mahon's uncannily responsive vision of place is inseparable from his awareness of writers and artists who have helped define them. The poet of 'Lives' is always fascinated by 'The Lives of Others', and the same is true of his representations of cities, which are invariably filtered through the eyes of others: with the Paris of 'Resistance Days' viewed via French photographers,

Sartre, and de Beauvoir; 'Rue des Beaux Arts' via the exiled Wilde; the Rome of 'Roman Script' through the poetry and cinema of Pasolini; and the Manhattan in 'New York Time' is mediated through a host of transient poets, painters, novelists, and cinematographers. In the same way, it is through Bashō that 'The Snow Party' conjures its charged image of Japan's cities, with 'silence / In the houses of Nagoya / And the hills of Ise'. Though some readers recoil from Mahon's experiments with the long poem in *New York Time* and 'Decadence', these exposed and innovative 1990's sequences were written in response to unprecedented economic and cultural crises within the global metropolis in the latest *fin-de-siècle*, and the battle to represent them is registered in the battered urbanity of their form.

Looking back over his long journey from the childhood Belfast of 'Glengormley' to the Co. Cork of his last five collections, I am struck by the exhilarating mobility and intellectual agility of Mahon's vision – the sheer variety of subjects, objects, places, and people it embraces. The range mirrors that of the often dazzlingly eclectic prose of *Journalism*, *Red Sails*, and *Olympia and the Internet*, and the dazzling translations of poets from Homer to Houellebecq in *Echo's Grove*. Mahon's cosmopolitan embrace is sometimes read as a reaction to the cultural restrictiveness of his native Northern Ireland, embalmed in the early 'Ecclesiastes', but it also offered a salutary corrective to the inward gaze of much Irish poetry after Yeats. A crucial part of his legacy is the sense that, after Mahon, Irish poets can write about absolutely anything. The world's their oyster.

Mahon's oeuvre, like MacNeice's, is 'incorrigibly plural', but it is also singularly concerted and mediated by his signature intellectual *cantabile*. This remains true of his last collection, *Washing Up*. Some readers may miss the alienated critical intensity and sheer polish of *The Snow Party* and *The Hunt by Night*, but the range of subjects and stanzaic forms is as exhilarating as ever. As in *Against the Clock*, Mahon is content to be the laureate of Kinsale, writing poems such as 'Around the Town' and 'Around the House', or 'Among the Rocks', celebrating the domestic world he shares with his partner Sarah Iremonger, and the local world where (in the triple-rhymed expanding tercets used in 'Craigvara House'): 'we survive / not in the urban hive / but far away, in touch with wind and wave' ('Open Air'). He continued to write the poems of our climate to the end.

In his Faber selection of Swift's poems, Mahon called his gift 'eminently situational', and the same is true of Mahon, whether confronting our planetary ecological crisis, 'strip mining and data mining' in 'Atlantis', or railing against the Dublin poetry world in 'After Swift', where he fingers '*Bailey* who gives me bad reviews'. Against these, and the 'high-rising town', Mahon offers an ironic portrait of the artist as an old man in drily rhymed tetrameters:

Just so, in such wasteful hours
I'd squander my declining powers,
for ever thinking of this sober
work table above the harbour.
Here in my quiet inglenook
I doze or read a serious book
ignoring, in reflective slowth
the world of economic growth.
— 'AGAINST SWIFT'

Work tables as scenes of writing have always played an important role in Mahon, but that witty celebration of both the 'work table' and 'reflective slowth' goes to the heart of the new book, and its buoyant combination of political critique and lyrical affirmation of a postmodern romantic aesthetic attuned to the natural world around him, and what he calls 'the elemental afterlife'.

If Mahon is a great poet of place, it is because he has such a complex, multiple sense of it being simultaneously local and expansive, framed in global and planetary terms. 'Washing Up' is an intensely personal poem about doing the dishes at the sink, but goes on to speak of 'Knowing our own place, I infer / from my perspective as *plongeur* / in the whole turbulent shebang.' It morphs into one of his many poems about the climate emergency, speaking of 'so much washing up to do / on the degraded planet now – / oceans and forests, oily sands, / our filthy-lucrative demands / on the resources of this place'. It is this multi-focal agility that gives Mahon's eco-poetry its force. The title poem is one of many to juggle the personal and planetary, including its companion piece 'Dust', which starts out defending the 'careful chaos' of his writing desk and 'the ash / I drop with nonchalant panache' against being dusted, before moving to embrace the need for renewal, asking what happens to all the dust which 'blows away like sand or snow / but then regroups and merges with / the live components of the earth.' It ends with a quasi-biblical vision of first and last things:

See that block of apartments? Dust.
Manhattan Equity and Trust?
Dust; and to dust all these return.
It's from the dust that we were born.

Something comparable is at work in 'Sand', which imagines pouring sand into 'complex systems' while listening for the sound of 'engines seizing up / and shuddering to a stop.' Such poems are small-scale complex systems themselves, composed in response to the turbulent and destructive complex systems they set themselves against, with a poem called

'Natural Resources' followed by 'Natural Selection', a poem which is equally about trees and the displacement of one human generation by another. Beside a tripartite ode to 'Algae', Byronically rhymed with 'nostalgia', there is a poem called 'Atlantis' which sketches a parabolic *Brave New World*-style account of a technological modernist Utopia morphing into an ecological dystopia which ends: 'It will be fabulous and will cost the earth.'

One of the most hauntingly personal poems is called 'Alone in the Dark', and has the poet waiting for his partner to return from 'a girls' night out' as he can just make out 'the glimmering white paper where I write / by the bright radiance of a single star', striving 'to check / routine emergence of an old dislike / for the triumphant kitsch on every side.' While realising that 'The only sure escape is to be dead', he resolves to 'ignore the latest news, / the opinion pieces, and take longer views', and apostrophises a Keatsian 'Bright star' to 'help me broadcast the poetic word'. As always, however, Mahon is never only alone in the dark in his poems. Stepping away from the world, he remains intensely aware of it. He may turn to the blank page, stars, and Keats's 'poetic word', but these poems also respond to 'opinion pieces' and the 'latest news', as in 'Quarantine', his last poem published in *Poetry Ireland Review*. There, he confronts our Coronavirus crisis, reflects on 'Bad news, though, from abroad: so many / stricken, and buried with scant ceremony', and in doing so calls ups 'The privileged crowd in the *Decameron*' and Camus's *La Peste* (rhymed with 'the past'). The poem ends characteristically with 'a briny stench ... from the roaring shore', grounding us in Kinsale, but only after a plague *tour du monde*. *Washing Up* is as full of poems about other writers and artists as earlier Mahon books, including sonnets on black-and-white movies and US writers, and numerous Romantics, including Byron, Moore, Verlaine, and Schubert and his 'final work of quiet *Sturm und Drang* / each song a swan song from the dark.'

Mahon remains impenitently 'literary' to the end. His tastes may be eclectic and cosmopolitan, but such dialogues with the dead are a way of engaging with the present. In 'Diary Extract (Late T'ang)', for example, Mahon adopts the persona of a classic Chinese nature poet, who speaks of re-dedicating 'our brushes to the fine art of poetry'. The poem is full of brief notes on wildlife ('Walked in the forest: goldfinch in a bush, / hawk on a thermal, pheasants in undergrowth'), but sets its painterly dream of 'ideal country' against a dissonant vision of empires that 'whatever their proclaimed virtues, / succumb to age, invasion, viruses' (and that slide from 'virtues' to 'viruses' is unnerving). The speaker aligns himself with Li Po's 'sure instinct for the longer view', and such literary masks and borrowings not only create a sense of intellectual company in a dark time, but of cultural survival, comparable to the Darwinian resilience of the inherited rhymed stanza forms he plays upon. They also reflect Mahon's undiminished 'instinct for the longer view'.

Jorge Luis Borges once wrote that:

> A man sets himself the task of portraying the world. Through the years he peoples a space with images of provinces, kingdoms, mountains, bays, ships, islands, fishes, rooms, instruments, stars, horses, and people. Shortly before his death, he discovers that the patient labyrinth of lines traces the image of his face.

This is true of Mahon. I don't think any modern poet has offered a more wide-ranging and complex portrait of their contemporary world, or shown greater lyric agility than the poet of 'The Globe in Carolina', 'Courtyards in Delft', and 'Washing Up'. He has peopled his poems with images of cities, ports, and seaside towns from all over the place; with stars, rivers, and planets; rooms, streets, and restaurants; rivers, beaches, and woods; paintings, photos, and movies; writers, artists, and musicians; friends, enemies, and intimates. His poems offer long views of the lives of things (as in 'Lives') as well as of things in our lives, like the potatoes celebrated in the new Donne-like metaphysical poem 'Spuds in Space', which notices that their 'surface is like ours / in texture, the peculiar bumps, the eyes', and praises the way their 'moist interior breathes / a fresh scent of the earth', and culminates in a cosmic vision of the night sky's 'twinkling farms, starlit / potato fields as far as the eye can reach.' If his poems trace the image of his own face and provide a unique self-portrait in Borges's sense, taken together they are a dazzling instance of what Stevens calls 'Poems of Our Climate'. In every sense.

Frank Farrelly

JOURNEY TO THE BOILER ROOM

One night, about ten years ago, in The Cove Bar, Waterford, I showed a poem to my poet-friend, Edward Denniston. He read it, made some encouraging suggestions, and pronounced: "There is a poem there – somewhere."

I demurred, studied it carefully, then caved in. It *was* hastily penned, lazily formed – my words, not Edward's. Stung into action, a week later I presented a better, revised version. Pride was restored. After that, there was no going back. I threw myself into my writing with more vigour, more patience, and most thrillingly of all, a sense of fulfilment. Later that same year, another poem, my first published one, appeared in *THE SHOp* magazine.

I started attending workshops and poetry festivals. Soon my poems were widely published, and placed in competitions. Jane Clarke adjudged me the winner of The Rush Poetry Prize in 2017. Although I harboured no ambition other than to continue to write, and to interact with those similarly afflicted, and although I always believed that 'It is better to travel hopefully than to arrive', before I knew it, I was flirting with the notion of a first collection. Was there a book there too – 'somewhere'?

I knew I was late to the game, only taking up writing 'seriously' in my early fifties, by which time I had a considerable crop of life's wheat and chaff to separate. And though I had lost much of youth's impetuousness, I retained some of its spontaneity. I was sixty-four when *The Boiler Room* came out. Rilke said, 'Poems amount to so little when you write them too early in your life.' That's my excuse. To everything there is a season.

There are turning points. Being selected by the wonderful Martina Evans for Poetry Ireland Introductions Series, 2019 (awarded to 'emerging' poets, even at sixty-three!) was a great boost to my self-belief. Martina urged, 'Keep writing your poems.' I did, but I also paused to gather my forces, as it were, to go about the business of finding a permanent home for some of my ten years' work.

Already, I had produced a pamphlet, *Close to Home*, in 2017, thanks to a Literary Bursary from Waterford Artlinks, following a Mentoring Programme with Grace Wells. Artlinks also awarded me a Residency Bursary for The Tyrone Guthrie Centre at Annaghmakerrig, where I spent a very stimulating and productive week.

Where to start? I chose about sixty poems, making sure to include many previously published, and those that had featured in competitions. I printed them out and spread them on the floor. This helped me to sift, categorise, to pair and sequence them. I sought a linking theme, some connecting thread, and found three. I arranged the collection in three unequal parts; 'Kith and Kin' (family, childhood); 'Place of Learning' (adolescence, teaching experience); 'In Adversity' (conflict in private / public spheres).

The poems were sequenced chronologically, wherever possible, and / or desirable. I found this an effective organising principle, and whether by accident or design, no poem exceeded one side of a page. I made a short-list of 'book title' contenders and asked a few friends for their favourite. In the end, I ditched the shortlist and decided on a poem in the collection, 'The Boiler Room'. It's theme of family was central to the collection's spirit, and it had an edginess that appealed to me, suggestive of creative energy, heat, regulation, and control of human passions.

I sent a copy of the manuscript to a few writing friends, as my 'early read-ers', who might have some suggestions. That done, I made any necessary revisions. Then I spoke to a friend, Maureen Curran, who had recently published with Revival Press, and she suggested I send my manuscript to them. (It was from Maureen's first collection, *Home*, that I got the initial idea for the three subdivisions in my own collection.)

I was thrilled when Revival Press editor, Dominic Taylor, agreed to publish *The Boiler Room*. I sent the manuscript to three poets, who were happy to provide a blurb for the back cover. I also organised a decent head shot. My artist daughter, Ali, designed the stunning cover art.

The online launch took the form of a Zoom interview, during the Water-ford Writers Weekend, 2020, and was conducted by Richard Hayes, who guided the ship home in great style. When the book finally reached my hands, I experienced a mixture of relief, joy, and achievement that I will never forget.

Niamh NicGhabhann

EACH OTHER'S LIVES

Pádraig J Daly, *A Small Psalter* (Scotus Press, 2020), €12.
Eamon Grennan, *Plainchant* (The Gallery Press, 2020), €11.95.
Kerry Hardie, *Where Now Begins* (Bloodaxe Books, 2020), £9.95.
Julie O'Callaghan, *Magnum Mysterium* (Bloodaxe Books, 2020), £10.99.

The title of Pádraig J Daly's latest collection, *A Small Psalter*, creates a
direct link between his work and a tradition of sacred poems and songs,
and in particular to the blend of solemnity, joy, and protest found in the
psalms. While the author has prefaced his own psalter with the word
'small', this is a book that ranges from Dublin's Liberties to the starry
heavens. It opens with a cluster of preliminary materials – a passage on
religious individualism and toleration by Jack Harte, quotations from
John Locke and Thomas Merton, and a line-drawing of King David at
his lyre or harp. These prefatory materials allude to both ecstasy and
ignorance, to the joyous celebration of the known and the awe of the
unknowable.

Several poems throughout *A Small Psalter* reflect on this core theme
of wonder. In 'World', Daly 'Gasps at this taken-for-granted world / And
our place in it.' 'Déisibh Mumhan' is a beautiful series of vignettes set in
the Ardmore cliffs, with Daly charting his own experience of ecstatic
observation of the natural world:

> For mere minutes the cloud lifted
> And the sun spread wide across strand and sea.
> I was glad when mists came down.
> I could not have borne the splendour longer.

While the tradition of writing about the natural world as a reflection of
the divine is a venerable one, *A Small Psalter* also occupies an interesting
position within the environmental humanities and contemporary
environmental theology, reflecting the urgency of Pope Francis's 2015
Laudato Si encyclical letter on care for our common home. In 'Aos Óg',
the young are observed walking home 'Answering phones, distracted by
gadgets', while 'they and all their artefacts / And all on earth and all the
fiery stars // Are plunged in God.'

The title poem of the collection is a meditation on the poet's own
faith and vocation, and his process of reflection on this particular life
path makes up a substantial part of the book, including 'A Celibate Life'
and 'Novices: Orlagh Revisited'. Daly is strongest when writing from

this place of personal experience, rather than the poems in the book that imagine the interior lives of others. The image of the 'Triune God, inhabiting the deep of us, / Reassembling the broken chaneys of the mind' ('A Small Psalter') is a resonant one, with its picture of shards hidden in the clay. Like the original psalms, this is a diverse book, with several translations from early-modern Irish poems included, reflecting Daly's keen attention to rhythm and word choice, allowing the rich, rough-hewn texture of the poems to be revealed.

Eamon Grennan's *Plainchant* also seems to align itself with the world of religion, and its emphasis on attentiveness and close observation of the natural world has an accord with Daly's collection. In 'Entering Omey with Rachel and Kira', for instance, Grennan closes the poem with 'a foot- / crushed clump of chamomile to release its scent like / a blessing of incense to us where we stand in the / ordinary, daily-changing, everlasting island air.' Like Daly, Grennan works to communicate a sense of the sacred moment, the observed world as it passes. In this, perhaps, they are both followers of William Carlos Williams's red wheelbarrow in the rain, using the poem as a space for sensation, witness, and account. However, the source of wonder in *Plainchant* is in the natural world itself, rather than a reflected deity. According to *Grove Music Online*, plainchant is defined as the official monophonic unison (originally unaccompanied) of the Christian liturgy. Grennan's collection of prose poems, each roughly a paragraph-page in length, is akin to this particular chant style, eschewing formal structure for a more direct register. Like plainchant, however, Grennan builds structure and repetition into each piece, with word combinations creating distinctive rhythmic patterns. The first poem in the book, 'Encounter', opens with this direct, falling staccato: 'Knacky keen and swift was the flighty hare / that flitted almost up to me in Fogarty's / near field'.

For the most part, the poems in *Plainchant* take the form of a paragraph-length sentence, structured throughout with punctuation marks like commas, em-dashes, and semi-colons, but appearing as a single rush of observation and expression. These punctuation marks often act as wayfinders for the reader, signalling turning points or shifts in perspective, and sometimes creating a space between images. The majority of the poems focus on the poet's experience of the West of Ireland landscape and wildlife, and are redolent of the sonic and visual richness of that environment, from the 'hazeblue fretworked silhouette of Achill' ('How Things Add Up'), to the 'big cob with great loud water-slapping wingflaps [...] the / sound of his beating wings above my head was not a bell- / beat no, but a series of sharp explosive reports as of huge / hands clapping an old slow dance of their own untaught / devising' ('Renvyle Couple'). The sheer volume of observed detail, together with the prose-poem style and the poet's use of composite words throughout (i.e., 'long-legged, / brown-feathered, curve-beaked' ('With Curlews and Starlight'), 'grey-opaque / rain-thickened swirl-about air' ('Singer in Storm'), can seem diffuse and overwhelming at times. By contrast, Grennan's use of sharper imagery elsewhere builds compelling, memorable, and vivid pictures of this environment, from the 'Little lethal goldbeaks' of 'Tangle', to 'Rain Cows':

> Silent and stolid and sullen-looking under the spilling rain these
> six cows have made a mucky black mash of the field path again

'Real Estate' is a short poem at the heart of Kerry Hardie's latest collection:

> For thirty years
> we have walked around
> inside each other's lives.
>
> We pay bills, hang out the wash,
> comfort children who wake.
> Sometimes we bury our dead.

This distilled image of a relationship, of points of independence and inter-dependence, is one that recurs throughout *Where Now Begins*. The poem closes with a final stanza: 'This is the room we inhabit, / fragile as glass, / the light passing through.' Hardie's poems chart a series of moments within relationships – of misunderstandings, last opportunities, and missed connections. Poems like 'Last Swim', 'Too Late for Sorry Now', and 'Talking to My Stepson' are poised between memory and regret: 'What's done stays done forever. / I understand this now and it's too late.' This exploration of relationships is clear-eyed, allowing for irresolution rather than tidy endings, as reflected in the final lines of 'Shasta Daisies': 'and me thinking of families and the hell / of that locked writhing and wishing that none of it / had ever happened at all / but now that it's all come apart, I'm left wondering – '.

Throughout, Hardie draws powerful images of these foundational relationships throughout the life cycle. In 'Shopping', 'arms full of melting vanilla', the speaker recalls a final holiday and the losses of dementia. In 'Escapology', the poet's wish for her mother's release into death is a 'cat's-cradle tangle of needs, / from my box with its blindfolds and bonds.' In 'Taking the Weight', a father's coffin is lowered into the ground. The loss of a sister is described as 'The link in the chain that's wrenched open; / your link falling loose' ('The Inadequacy of Letters of Condolence'). The simple, direct clarity of 'Permission' acts like an anchor for these different explorations of life, grief, and death: 'to live with this knowledge / and not to try to avoid it.' As well as Hardie's concern with relationships, *Where Now Begins* examines the interior life of the individual, and the ways in which a sense of self is forged in the contexts of circumstance and environment. These explorations range from the confrontation between the self and the expanse of the world (as in 'Blasted' – 'No roof to my house, empty stars'), and 'Time Passing', to an encounter in a range of significant landscapes and spaces – Gallarus Oratory, 'A yellow house that's patched and stained' ('How She Disposes of Fear'), a winter solstice interior, and a sand dune.

Hardie also invokes an elemental sense of religion, from 'The old saints roar for the new young saints', in 'All Saints'; the 'clutch and tell' of beads in 'Winter Solstice'; and a striking image of prayer in 'Into Light':

> as brief and intense
> as a coal-tit's fierce cling
>
> to a coconut strung from ash in the rainy air.

The title of Julie O'Callaghan's collection, *Magnum Mysterium*, comes from the Holy Matins of Christmas, describing the animals in wonder as they observe the Christ child. The 'great mystery' of the world described by O'Callaghan eschews sentimental registers, however, and from the opening poems the reader encounters the gap between the glory of the world and the limited capacity of the human to navigate its sphere.

In the opening poem, 'Island Life', 'Water sloshes uncontrollably / at the edges', and 'You can hardly / go anyplace / without falling off', while in 'Voyage', Magellan is lost, anxious about falling off the edge of the planet, but cautiously hopeful. These images of navigating potential danger, of things unseen or beneath the surface, appear throughout, as in 'Zen Christmas', 'Ship', and 'Horse Power'. In several poems in this collection, O'Callaghan combines surrealism with a pointed use of language. In 'Riddle', for example, holy functions are matched with bell sounds:

> sings a wedding   cling
> prays vespers   blang
> cries holy blessings   blong

The closing lines of 'Stay' also marry sharp simplicity and surrealism: 'You get up off this rock / and fly away. / I get up off this rock / and stay.'

The final section of the book comprises a series of poems 'After Dennis O'Driscoll', and this is a wry, clear-eyed, and powerful exploration of life after great loss. The images of unsteadiness and of a dangerous world, difficult to navigate, that appear in the early part of the book, resurface here. In 'Beyond', the speaker in the poem is 'here in the ocean / surrounded by sea monsters', and in 'My Limit', the act of walking around the city of Dublin becomes overwhelming: 'I tried it yesterday / and had to grab a building / to stop myself falling / or spontaneously combusting / or crouching in a doorway'. In 'Here', the speaker has 'crash-landed on a planet', while 'Alien' describes a 'wrong impossible place'. In this section, O'Callaghan communicates a sense of total loss which is impossible to out-run, with interior, exterior, and even cyber spaces all entirely full of grief and symbols of loss. In 'Me & Our House', she writes that 'not one of these / PhDs or Popes or Astrophysics experts // can solve the problem / of me & our house // moping for you'. O'Callaghan both skewers the insufficiency of poetic comforts in the face of grief ('you're clomping / around on my dreams' ('Dreams'), but also measures the individual experience against a cosmic scale: 'But the Angel of the Lord / shakes its head and sayeth: / Get over yourself' ('Faith').

O'Callaghan brings an extraordinarily painful tenderness to certain images – the boxes of personal papers, leaving the home to be transferred to an archive, are described in 'It'll Be OK':

> FEDEX will be here soon.
> The boxes stand quietly in the hallway
> like little kids wearing hats and scarves
> waiting nervously to go somewhere
> they aren't that thrilled about.
> I tell them it'll be OK.

Compared to the images of Gulliver and Magellan that open the book, this terrain of grief seems to be the most daunting journey of all to map as it unfolds.

Stephen Sexton

ON PUBLISHING A FIRST BOOK

The path to what became my first book, *If All the World and Love Were Young*, was both perfectly typical and not so typical. My biography as a writer bears many hallmarks of contemporary poets, for better or worse: I did an English degree, followed by a master's degree and a Ph.D.; publishing along the way – or aiming to – poems here and there in magazines and journals, including, I say gratefully, this one. Debates are frequent and intense, I know, when it comes to poets in academia or, what's more to the point, I think, academia in poetry. I see both sides of the argument.

In 2011, I started an M.A., and found at Queen's University, Belfast, a community of poets and writers who were committed to the art with considerable and occasionally overwhelming intensity. The rhythm of reading, writing, and poetry workshops became a thrill, as did the negotiations of temperaments and ambitions and styles, as did the many poetry nights and open mics, magnificent and unbearable. These have practical and enduring real-world applications, but it's the feeling of being part of a community of people working towards similar goals that became inescapably important for me.

Michael Longley described the writing community in Belfast in the 1960s as a kind of 'convection current': one person's success resulted in the kind of upward draft which simultaneously brought others along and encouraged them to up their game. More than anything else, this context and practise of reading and writing gave me the confidence to take myself seriously as someone who writes poems. The Lifeboat Reading Series was started by Stephen Connolly and Manuela Moser in Belfast in 2012 and it celebrated local and emerging writers (and all other gradations of esteem and longevity), and attracted many other good-willed people who were visiting or were willing to travel. Thanks to this and other institutions, such as Mary Denvir's legendary Bookfinders Café, we were immersed in poetry. By the end of my M.A. in 2012, I couldn't be without this society and culture, so I found a way to a Ph.D.

During this time, I started publishing poems with a little more intention. Publication strategies seem to be various. I knew of people who always had work out and under consideration, amending or redirecting what was rejected. I never had enough poems I liked to be able to do that. Moreover, once and once only, a very poor poem was published in a journal and I cringed for months afterwards. As a consequence, I found myself being much more selective with which poems I sent to which magazine or editor, and much harder on myself. Naturally, 'prestige' is an immensely complicated tangle of privilege and funding and history, but a poem in a prestigious journal tends to be more effectual than five poems in less prestigious journals. Mostly, I wanted more of that convection current, so I aimed my work towards publications at the upper end of my aspirations.

In 2013, The Emma Press, a small press in London, published a poem in an anthology. I still remember the thrill of surreptitiously reading the acceptance e-mail on the 'floor' of the call-centre job I was doing (security breach). This led to an invitation to publish a pamphlet, which I gleefully accepted. In 2014, *Oils* was published. My experience of poetry publishing has been, broadly, that one demonstrates something like commitment or seriousness by first publishing poems, then a pamphlet (or an EP, as I like to think of it), then a collection (LP), often collecting together many of these published poems. This route is what's become typical over the last twenty years or so, partly due to the structure and culture of poetry prizes. This is by no means the only approach, I understand very well, but it's largely been mine.

So far, so typical. The only significant deviation I took from this method is that of not publishing a collection. 'Poetry Collection' and 'Poetry Book' are pretty much synonymous terms, but they're not the same thing. *If All the World and Love Were Young* is not a collection in the literal sense: none of these poems were collected together to be published as a book. My first book is more of 'project book'; something more common in the US than Ireland. I think of it as a concept album. Has this decision made a difference? I can't be sure. There's something novel, you might agree, about a first collection being a second book. *Cheryl's Destinies* will be published in August 2021. I'll report back.

Declan Ryan

CRAFTY

Alan Gillis, *The Readiness* (Picador, 2020), £10.99.
Justin Quinn, *Shallow Seas* (The Gallery Press, 2020), €11.95.

In Alan Gillis's finely-tuned 'Tollymore', we encounter a speaker
'crouched in conifer shadow, / green-golden reeds, butterstreaks of light, /
still in the moment though all sways / in motion' – time collapsing to the
tune of 'The happy-sad chorus of an ice-cream van', a whiff of soap suds
implicit if not uttered as 'in a flash the forty years / stream out to sea'. A
number of the most convincing aspects of Gillis's latest collection, *The
Readiness*, bring with them echoes of Louis MacNeice, whether in the
sudden reverie above or the occasional use of a chorus, or coda,
deployed with particular élan in 'Lament for a Long Day in the Lonely
Estates', where a phrase from Jules Laforgue – 'You go away and leave
us / you leave us and you go away' – becomes a sort of marching song
for the daily removal from home at the heart of many of the poems, a
sense of withdrawal and – usually eager – return their abiding motion. If
these moments have something of MacNeice's classical poise, a louder,
more syncopated music is made elsewhere, with Gillis plunging into an
at-times squeamish-making onomatopoeia, turning up the sonic effects
and wielding a showy, sometimes demotic lexicon with menaces.
    A poem such as 'Before the Bustle of Day' – another taking off from
the increasingly alien-seeming routine of leaving one's house in the
morning – ricochets with qualifiers and showy verbs, characterful in
isolation but verging, in bulk, on overwhelming: 'schlong', 'squinches',
'squiggle', 'whigmaleeries' – the risk of this consonantal bombardment
is of bringing a surface top-heaviness to the poem, which finally resolves
itself on a well-behaved, prosaic note, 'today will be what we make of it',
having taken a brief diversion into the sort of echoingly avuncular chimes
found in recent TV adverts:

> Sizing up the right shoes, left shoes, controversial issues,
> medicinal doses,
> runny noses, mirrored poses ...

At their best, Gillis's blending of registers, his propulsive assonances, give
his lines rhythmic swagger, but in less freewheeling moments these pyro-
technics occlude the poems in which they're – heavily – deployed:
'Scaffolding' and 'The Way to a Man's Heart' struggle to climb far
beyond being vehicles for their interesting word choices, for example

– which makes a poem such as 'The Interior', with its bald statement 'There are no adjectives', doubly enticing. A fascinatingly pared-down tone, at once meditative and disquieting, emerges through the creeping depiction of a room, dawning in description and accumulation of detail, creating a freshness to a voice which has, in some of the noisier poems, verged on calcifying into a comfortably rote delivery, thick with end-rhymes and welcoming of the ephemera in a mostly urban, technology-laden, environment.

There are several longer poems, landing somewhere between the sequence and the suite. 'Vespers' closes the show with a winning energy and sweeping shots of night-time in the neighbourhood; there's a charged interiority and feeling to some of its description and snapshot scenes, sometimes missing amid the clatter elsewhere. An especially well-observed moment of marital yearning pulls us up: 'wishing, one night, she'd undress / out of her newfangledness // to suede and swathe him in the rain / of her hair.' The softer echoes of 'suede and swathe', the halting sibilance, work niftily with the heavy end-rhyme to show Gillis's ear at its best. 'Metropolis' seems less sure of its intentions, talking itself into a cul-de-sac, caught between being a hard-boiled detective narrative and a check-box of Internet phraseology, via Marx quotations and a surprising cameo from Gary Lineker. Gillis's verve and selection of the clinching detail seems to serve him best on the slightly shorter-haul journeys, and a poem such as 'On Blackford Hill' feels like something of a sweet spot, roomy enough for him to weave a narrative but with enough compression to prevent any loss of momentum, its mentions of 'the thisness of the air' suggestive of something true throughout the collection's sharpest images, their carefully noticed particularities.

There's an admirable variety of approach here, with narrative, tall-tale, and dystopian fable all competing for attention, and a willingness to fore-ground the singing line; well-made poems such as opener and title poem 'The Readiness' are a useful reminder of Gillis's *bona fides* as a craftsman. The quieter moments may hint at a slow reformulation of style, or may simply be breathers or outliers, but it's in those more reined-in poems of memory, contemplation, and – without sounding too wearily monastic – minor self-denial that Gillis most intrigues, for all the bombast and aural filigree elsewhere.

'Heart Song', one of the finest poems in Justin Quinn's new collection *Shallow Seas*, sees human and deer in a somewhat co-dependent bind, the deer 'lays down beats to do with dying and sex, / beats I can't hear (I only hear my own).' There's a quickened pulse to the performance here, something important is at stake – sex, death – and the whole scene takes place on the verge of breathlessness, the brief communion liable to collapse on a hair-trigger reflex. The speaker is similarly fraught and edgy, 'I take my pills years after it has gone / and hang around here try-ing to catch the words', unsure and – to some extent – imperilled, albeit not by hunters' guns. The poem operates at a level of intensity often absent elsewhere, its amped-up mood and ticking clock the ideal counter-balance to Quinn's calmly resolving pentameters, his default of the well-ordered stanza, the polished rhyme.

By contrast, the opening poem 'Platform', in fourteen numbered parts, is perhaps a strange one to begin with, its 'long years of non-event. / / And nothing happened here' not quite its whole story but not far off; a narrative of property development and gentrification coming out of the distant historical past, its early seeding in of a cooling corpse hinting we might have been in for something more mysterious or implicating than what emerges. A similar note of well-ordered but slightly cold-blooded dexterity is struck across the collection – Quinn has an unerringly deft knack for turning a line, for shaping a stanza, but all too often puts his skill at the service of poems which best satisfy through their shape, their construction, rather than a conjunction of architecture and substance. That's not to say each poem has to operate at a lip-trembling pitch of emotion, but the contrast with some of Quinn's own best work – a collection such as Close Quarters (2011) – is notable, the artisanal turning out of a sequence such as 'Street Weeds' smacking more of the exercise than anything in that earlier, more insistent book.

Similarly, the closing poem 'The Metals', another long, numbered sequence, passes by in a wave of noticed backgrounds and relatively lightly-worn research, detailing the engineering, construction, and industry around the waters of Quinn's native Dublin, but only resolving itself into something like his perceptive, felt best in part 16: 'shocked / when cold saltwater swathed us in itself, / but getting used to it, splashed and rocked, / we struck out further on the sinking shelf.' In that moment there is something more vitally forceful going on, a clarifying pulse and charge working in unison with the subtle patterning and music, the poem's song aligning with its mood, cohering into compelling electricity after so much calmly nimble plotting.

There are other poems which marry their metres to an odd brio. 'Eight Radioactive Tableaux (with Venus and Adonis)' is a pleasingly weird mix of radiation and ekphrasis, while 'Jerome' utilises the language of the CIA's interrogative alertness with the life of Saint Jerome to create something charming and unexpected, a lion standing as an avatar for the unknown, the foreign, and the blending of histories giving Quinn's stepped stanza a re-energised strut, allowing his use of rhyme to pick up the felicities and surprising associations which, at its best, the method encourages. A committed, easeful formalist, Quinn's fidelity to some-times certain-seeming rhyme schemes is rarely to his detriment, such is his ability to work across the patterning and adapt his stresses and syntax, but there are a few moments when an unrelenting stricture feels more strait-jacket than accomplice, not least in 'Oak Song', a monologue in the tree's voice where 'show him' rhymes with 'phloem' and 'Dude' with 'food'. If the tone of the collection is, on the whole, a slightly sedate or warily remote one, we might be grateful one lurch into something lighter and more humorous proves a rarity, if 'Child of Prague' is its touchstone:

> You don't hang round for the applause, your boogie shoes
> are moving quicker than the videos upload.

There is, frustratingly, a sense of undercurrent, so much unspoken as to be almost inaudible – to the collection's detriment. It threatens to peek through: in 'Dresden Therapy Maenad', the speaker feels 'ripped open', we are told, but not necessarily shown; and the promising opening of 'Adelsö', with its unavoidable echoes of James Wright ('I am lying in a hammock in Sweden'), devolves into a poem of plucky self-motivation, a sense that 'we'll rise and clean up last night's plates and pots ... Anders Kotz / will brew another batch tomorrow', the sort of automatically willed crafting on show a little too often.

Proinsias Ó Drisceoil

SENSIBILITIES

Seán Ó Ríordáin, with translations by Greg Delanty, *Selected Poems: Apathy is Out/Rogha Dánta: Ní Ceadmhach Neamhshuim* (Bloodaxe Books, 2021), £12.99.
Fearghas MacFhionnlaigh, aistrithe go Gaeilge ag Simon Ó Faoláin, *A' Mheanbhchuileag/An Corrmhíol* (Coiscéim, 2018), €7.50.

The renowned translator Michael Hamburger once remarked of translators that they are at their most successful when they 'combine capacity to read with a capacity to write; and this quality of responsiveness to sensibilities other than their own seems much more essential ... than their linguistic qualifications.' This statement both challenges and encourages translators such as Greg Delanty, translator of the present volume and a renowned US-based poet, who, as he readily reveals in the introduction, has 'poor' Irish and was dependent on cribs from the late Liam Ó Muirthile as a way into Seán Ó Ríordáin's poetry. (Delanty and Ó Muirthile share Ó Ríordáin's Cork background.)

Ó Ríordáin's poetry often contains newly-coined compound words, but his Irish otherwise employs an everyday idiomatic register. In this respect, the originals often contrast sharply with the Delanty translations, which, perhaps under American influence, frequently draw on an exotic word-store intended, presumably, to create a zany effect, as when the line from 'Oileán agus Oileán Eile' / 'An Island and Another Island', 'Chonac geanc is glún is cruit is spág', becomes 'I saw a stumpy snoz, knee, hump, and spawg.' This may be a nod to Ó Ríordáin's deadpan humour, as also with, for instance, 'off on his tod' for 'Ina aonar' ('Mise'/'Me'), but phraseology such as this, or the regular use of 'bloke' and 'chap', can cause the translations to lose contact with the register of the originals.

The translator of Ó Ríordáin faces a particular problem with the extent to which the English literary canon is a primary influence on Ó Ríordáin's poetry, an influence he sought to renounce, but one which was unsurprising in a modernist aesthetic for which Irish offered few precedents. If, in 'Fill Arís' / 'Return Again', Ó Ríordáin declares his intention of excluding Shelley, Keats, and Shakespeare from his work, the poems themselves, thankfully, contradict his anxiety at this influence. Thus, the lines 'Ní mhaireann cnoc dar chruthaigh Dia ann / Ach cnoic theibí, sainchnoic shamhlaíochta' ('Saoirse'/'Freedom') are clearly foreshadowed by Hopkins in 'No worst, there is none': 'O the mind, mind has mountains; cliffs of fall / Frightful, sheer, no-man-fathomed', and the translator must decide whether or not to draw attention to this debt.

Here, perhaps wisely, the translator decides to disregard the echoes and renders the second line as: 'only abstract hills, the range of the imaginary'.

As a translator, Delanty has a tendency to summarise rather than translate, as in the difficult line, 'A mheallfadh corp dom shamhailtghar-lach' ('A Sheanfhilí, Múinídh dom Glao'/'Old Poets, Show Us the Way'), given by Colm Breathnach in a previous book of Ó Ríordáin translations as 'that will bring form to my imagined urchin', but given here as 'entice it into my corpus', which, arguably, explains the line but does not trans-late it. Similarly, the sacramental overtones of 'faoistin' (confession) in the line, 'A mhalartóidh liom faoistin' ('Sos'/'Rest') are lost when the line is given as 'will confide in me'.

These translations are often rewarding poems in their own right, and attest to Delanty's abilities as a poet, but unresolved issues remain, as so often happens when going from a Celtic to a Germanic language.

Simon Ó Faoláin makes the apparently easier journey from Scottish to Irish Gaelic in his translation of Fearghas MacFhionnlaigh's long poem of 1980, 'A' Mheanbhchuileag' (translated by MacFhionnlaigh himself in 1982 as 'The Midge'). This, however, is a road with many misleading signposts and the very proximity of the two languages presents the translator with many dilemmas: difficulties arise, for instance, when the same word occurs in both languages, but where there are differences in overtone or levels of usage. An example of this is the word 'deò' (Scottish Gaelic for 'breath of air', 'glimmer', 'vital spark'), which occurs in Irish as 'dé', so that the translator, when dealing with the line 'Beò gun deò' (*alive without breath* or *vital spark*), has to decide whether or not to leave the line unaltered. The option chosen here is to transliterate, giving 'Beo gan dé', a perfectly valid approach, but one whose meaning may puzzle some Irish readers.

More innovative, if also more debatable, is his translation of the line, 'mar Leibhiatan eadar-dhà-lionn ann an cuan coimheach' (literally, *like a Leviathan faced with Hobson's choice in a strange sea*). This is given by Ó Faoláin as 'mar Leiviatan ag dul go tóin poill i bhfarraige chomh dubh le pic', literally 'like a Leviathan going to the bottom of a hole in a sea as black as pitch', a deviation from the original, but not a direct explanation.

This edition of the poem includes an introductory essay, written by MacFhionnlaigh and published here in Irish, in which he discusses many of the issues of politics, philosophy, and theology with which the poem is preoccupied. A wide range of intellectual influences, particularly the Calvinist theology of Herman Dooyeweerd, allow the poem to meander from questions of the divine to the quotidian and back again, engaging at length with Scotland's 'midge' weight in the world and, at the same time, its complicity in the British imperial project. MacFhionnlaigh's gift for imagery shines through on the imperial theme, as in these lines from

'The Midge', first published in 1982 in the journal *Cencrastus*:

> You chose captivity in the English zoo
> in order to avoid vulnerability.
> But you proved yourself so faithful
> that you were allowed to roam like a sheepdog
> (or was it rather like a doberman?)

Hugh MacDiarmid's 'A Drunk Man Looks at the Thistle', veering from insistent questions about man's existence to Scotland's troubled character, is a clear influence on 'A' Mheanbhchuileag', engaged as it is with our midge-sized individual significance. But 'A' Mheanbhchuileag' finds its principal context in the great tradition of the long Gaelic poem, extending from Alasdair Mac Mhaighstir Alasdair and Donnchadh Bàn Mac an tSaoir in the eighteenth century, to George Campbell Hay and Sorley MacLean in the twentieth, a tradition enriched by 'A' Mheanbhchuileag', a poem given an extended voice by this translation. Ó Faoláin, himself widely-published in Irish, succeeds in conveying the variable line length and speech-based rhythms of the original, and the result is a translation which is both readable and reliable.

Seosamh Ó Murchú

COGAR CAILLÍ

An chlagarnach obann úd ar an díon stáin
a d'fhógair go raibh an stoirm tagtha faoi

dheireadh; fágadh idir dhá chomhairle í
cé acu ab fhearr di faoiseamh nó fearg

a ghabháil chuici féin ar theacht na díle
mar b'amhlaidh gur ródhéanach a bhí

chun na barraí a chur ag fás ná chun
an saol mór eile a taibhríodh di aréir

a thabhairt ar phort bán a cuid aislingí
ná snáithíní tirime a croí a thaisriú

d'aithin sí an tséis á seimint ar an díon
bíodh is nárbh fhéidir di breith ar na nótaí.

Bríd Ní Mhóráin

IALUS
(Calystegia sepium)

Tréigeann dathanna, ceann ar cheann,
feileastram dearg, fraoch is feochadán;
Cránn an t-ialus an garraíodóir
ach is gile a splanc ná feo an Fhómhair.

Áine Ní Ghlinn

DROIM MO MHÁTHAR

Is cuimhin liom í is an taos á fhuinneadh is á fháscadh
aici. A droim i gcónaí linn is í ag obair léi sa chistin.

Císte á chur san oigheann. Gualainn bagúin ag dul isteach
sa phota ar an sorn. Prátaí á sciúradh sa bhuicéad stáin.

Is cuimhin liom sleamhnú isteach ina leaba is mé sceimhlithe
i ndiaidh tromluí. Í casta uaim is a haghaidh le balla.

Nuair a fuaireamar an teilifíseán shuíodh sí beagáinín beag
chun tosaigh orainn le bheith níos gaire don scáileán.

Agus í sa chónra rinne mé a haghaidh a iniúchadh ach chuaigh
sé sa mhuileann orm í a aithint.

Ceaití Ní Bheildiúin

SAOLÚ MHONGÁIN

Aisling a thugtar ar an ndán so
a thagann ag máinneáil as smugairle

na spéire, thar na farraigí
ina créatúr creathach, bodhar

ag glór na dtonn, cráite
ag an ngaoth is ag na faoileáin.

Cloistear Manannán ag guí
go scaoilfear saor í

thar an gcroí isteach.
I bpóca a chuimhne

chíonn sé cruinne oráiste
a d'fhás uair amháin ar a mhuin.

Fan agus tiocfaidh, a deir sé leis féin
is as na scamaill snámhann niamh.

Cloistear glaoch: Mac Manannáin slán!
Filleann bárc an tsamhraidh thar sáile,

an leanbh á sheoladh i dtír.
Siosarnach aduain ar an dtráigh,

mac altrama fé dheireadh thiar
thall ag Fiachna Mac Baodáin.

Tommie Lehane
Stroll

Tommie Lehane
Castle

Tommie Lehane
Sand dune

Tommie Lehane
Holidays

Tommie Lehane
Estella Solomon's secret garden

Tommie Lehane
Two hand reel

Tommie Lehane
Jump

Tommie Lehane
Ice lolly at training

www.tommielehane.ie

Simon Ó Faoláin

as AN CORRMHÍOL

An mbead beo amárach?
An rabhas beo riamh?
Táim buíoch
gur shlíocas cat.

Dúirt Giacometti tráth
dá mbeadh tine i ndánlann
go dtarrthálfadh sé cat roimh Rembrandt.
Fear críonna.
Ní scréachfadh pictiúr sna lasracha.

Bhí cat againn féin a fuair bás.
Tá's agam nach bhfuil sé cuí
cat a chaoineadh nuair a bhíonn
crith talún sa tSín,
agus tuilte sa Bhanglaidéis,
agus gorta fud leath an domhain.

Ach bhí cat againn a fuair bás.
Is bhí grá againn dhó.

      – Aistriúchán Gaeilge ar shliocht as *A' Mheanbhchuileag*
      le Fearghas MacFhionnlaigh

Máirtín Coilféir

PING

Píobaireacht chloigín a mhúscail, de bheagán,
As támhnéal de bhogcheo codlata mé
A tháinig anuas orm le lámha Steve –
Your masseur for the day
Sa só-spá, Sráid an Iarla –
Lámha síoda, go neartaí Dia iad,
Is iad a chuir faoin gceo mé
Agus sula raibh déanta acu de chaoin-
Trusláil mo mhothaill ghruaige
Níorbh ann ná leo a bhí mé níos mó,
Ach as, in áit éigin táimh,
Ag snámh liom go seoigh i scamall
Ar dhath na huibhe
Agus an scamall ag cur de liom
I monabar sámh
Agus d'airigh mé ann, más cruinn mo thomhas,
Glór athbhean uncal mo mháthar, de phór
Ghiúdaigh na Gearmáine
Go Nua-Eabhrac isteach
A deireadh gach focal riamh
Trína sróin.

Bobby Kohli, aithním thú! Agus
An cuimhin leat nuair a dúirt mé leat
(Nuair bhí tusa fós beo agus lán líon
De mhéara fós ar do chosa, agus mise
Deich mbliana, an lá a thug tú dhom
An chéad *massage* cinn dár bhlaiseas)
An cuimhin leat gur dhúirt mé le do ghob
Nach raibh d'oidhre ar do phéire liopaí
Ach liopaí sean-asail
Is sula raibh d'uain ag mo mháthair
A béal a chur ar dianleathadh,
Gurb sheo agam thú le do chuid
'Nára chosúla le cluasa sean-asail
Do phéire cluas mór-sa?'

Is agat a bhíodh an stopallán dhom
Is níor thuigeas go raibh tú
Airithe uaim chor ar bith agam
Gur dúisíodh mé ag cling
Chloigín taobh thiar dhíom.

Seán Lysaght

ROMANCE LANGUAGE

Cathal Ó Searcaigh, *Laoithe Cumainn agus Dánta Eile* (Arlen House, 2020), €15.

Writing a preface to a volume of his/her own poetry usually signals a particular ambition on the part of a writer: in this case, Cathal Ó Searcaigh's introduction to his new series of love songs sets out to align his work as a gay poet within the wider context of Gaelic tradition. Having given a number of modern writers their due as role models (Micheál Mac Liammóir, Pearse Hutchinson, and Micheál Ó Conghaile), he takes the search further, into the bardic tradition, and highlights the work of Eochaidh Ó hEoghusa (1558-1612), whose tributes to two aristocratic patrons, he argues, are so affectionate that they amount to a queering of classical poetry: 'is é mo bharúil féin gur chuir Eochaidh Ó hEoghusa cor cam sa Dán Díreach.' Here and elsewhere, Ó Searcaigh finds early examples of homosexual love: 'is dóigh liom… go bhfuil an ghné sin le sonrú go soiléir sa tsaothar.'

    Ó Searcaigh conducts his argument here with a zesty dash of humour, which deflects from a sense of the Irish bardic tradition being enlisted in a contemporary joust about sexual politics. The poems themselves, celebrating his early – and possibly greatest – love affair, are instantly recognisable as parts of a coherent sequence: discreetly numbered in Roman numerals, largely in quatrains with the second and fourth lines rhymed, and strong assonantal patterns.

    The opening line, 'A óganaigh an órfhoilt bhuí', echoes the title of a song in Scottish Gaelic which drove his inspiration, and it also connects with Irish poetry of the popular tradition, notably 'A ógánaigh an chúil cheangailte'. The quatrain plainly sets out the object and history of his passion:

> A óganaigh an órfhoilt bhuí
> a mbíodh lí na gréine i do ghruaidh,
> is tú is túisce a spreag mo dhúil
> is a chuir mé ag déanamh uabhair.

As the past tenses sweep with insistence through the second quatrain, the poet engages with another key theme: the memorialisation of their affair in poetry: 'thug mé buanaíocht duit i ndán / nuair a chan mé d'áilleacht is d'intinn ghrinn.' He takes this further, with a Platonic view of mortality as this first poem concludes:

Scéimh nach maireann a mheallann mé,
an luisne dhiaga i gcorp na cré.

With his keen instinct for compression in the opener, Ó Searcaigh has
tuned the pitch of the entire work. Several poems set the physical
relationship in the context of his Donegal landscape, both literally and as
a figuration of the body of the loved one. The third, short poem estab-
lishes the setting:

Cuimhneoidh mé ar an lá sin go brách,
boladh na raideoige ar an chosán go hAltán,
tusa le mo thaobh, aoibh na hóige ort,
is amhrán an tsrutháin ár dtionlacan sa chaorán.

Elsewhere, the connection with landscape is worked metaphorically,
as in the superb parallels between his lover and the moods of the sea in
the thirty-second piece. He imagines 'teangacha glasa na trá / ina chuid
cainte, suaitheadh na dtonn ag borradh / i ngile a gháire is i bhfarraigí
arda a ghrá.' Through a process recalling Keats's sonnet 'Bright Star',
the motion of the sea is animated by the energy of love-making, until a
climactic moment is reached, and the poet is overwhelmed:

sin an uair a thig a t-oibriú pléisiúrtha seo
i mo chéadfaí is téim sa tsáile de léim buile.

While the condition of loss and separation is made clear from the outset,
the poems alternate between present and past tenses. Even in the
celebratory present, there is an underlying awareness of mortality, as in
this quatrain (from 'XI'):

Inniu tá sé faoi ghnaoi is faoi aoibh na hóige,
amárach imeoidh an snua as a ghruaidh.
Níl seasamh ar bith i gcneas na cré,
mairg a chás is é ag cailleadh a ghné.

The sequence overall maintains its thematic coherence with a purity,
even an exclusivity, of diction. Language itself is venerated in exultant
patterns of assonance; Irish terms for earth and clay (cré, créafóg, úir), for
lustre and beauty (scéimh, luisne, gnaoi, aoibh), for desire and impulse
(dúil, craos, taom, buile) are relished through repetition and performance.
Ó Searcaigh keeps the currency of media-savvy Irish, with its loan words
and consumer labels, at a distance; in a parallel sense, there is little room
for the contemporary world in this exalted medium, and here I felt that
the poet's statements about modern oppression were out of kilter with

the cycle as a whole. The body itself, stripped of any attire, attains a kind of classical simplicity, where the veneration of the male body is comfortably at home. This aspect of the book is vividly captured by Seán Ó Gaoithín's excellent drawings, an extensive series of male figures accompanying the text and on the cover.

The stylistic impulse of purification goes hand in hand with the poet's address to the bards of classical tradition. Whereas he modestly offers his inadequacy at the altar of tradition ('níl ar mo chumas d'áilleacht a laoidheadh / le húdarás ná le dlús na bairdne', from 'IV'), he is nonetheless a disciple of their mastery, and the high tribute he pays to their excellence (in 'XVIII') reads very much like an audition for membership.

I think that *Laoithe Cumainn* measures up to its author's ambitions with a sustained performance in poetic language which manages to raise the idyll of an early romance into something approaching mythical status. By the end of the sequence, I felt that Ó Searcaigh's opening argument about gay writing in Irish had been superseded by a masterly achievement of classical poise.

Maria Stepanova

from THE BODY RETURNS

N

They lie, shot, in ravines filled with stars and bird cherry,
They lie in marshland, like dry stalks, like sprats in cans
They lie under banks, beneath lakes and autobahns
Beneath freerange grazing
Beneath sheep fields, where sheep go wild
Gainsaying any human part to this,

They lie under multistories
And runways
Where fingers of grass slit the paper-thin ice
Where blue signal lamps are cleverly placed
Where powerful bodies fly without our hands.

Where is my body, says the middle stratum
The earth's middle class: dead and still unresurrected.

M

And poetry speaks and knows what it says: I said
You are gods, I said, and all of you are children of the most High
But you shall die like fools:
Like one of the princes and generals
(politicians and aristocrats
and representatives of the swelling bourgeoisie)
Like mortals
Like nothing could be easier
Than the falling and the falling apart.
You die all the time
Like it was a normal thing to do.
Why don't you take yourselves in hand?
Why don't you make an effort,
Says poetry from under the ground, breathing through the hollow reeds.

L

Glory glory let's gather up this man
(scrape up the body like a lump of strawberry jam)

An eternal flame burns, it consumes the fallen
The unconsidered, undiscovered, the gone-before

Don't give up your cells to fire, your forty thousand cells
Or your nerve endings, or the fine nets of capillary walls

The ribbed palate, the pelvic down, the dusty pelvic floor
The slight partitions between the mind and ear

How will we gather them for Judgment Day?
Your bones didn't know they would be saved.

Sacks of seed, everything the body consumed
Iron – in our age becomes part of the exhumed

Body parts parts of another's body, which has lain here since another age
Together they make a new body
A not-yet-existent person.

K

Poetry, a many-eyed absurd
Nature of manymouths
Found in many bodies at the same time
Having lived in many other bodies before that
And now lying in confinement
Like something about to be born
(But at any moment an expedition of archaeologists
a curious shepherd
a dozen students in shorts
might pull you from the earth,
prematurely, not carried to full term,
and stick their fingers in your toothless gob)

Judging by the phosphorus content in the bone
English-speaking Poetry had a diet of fish.

J

They said, and it was confirmed by a graduate of the Theological
Institute, who quoted a doctoral thesis in support:

We will be resurrected as thirty-three-year-olds
Even those who died aged seventy or aged nine.

The body will know how to be resurrected
This is the body's privilege:

To eat and drink what it wants
To wander footsore many stadia
To wear upon its skin clothes, wounds, tears
To walk in water and evaporate into the air
To remain unrecognised, to make itself recognised
To resemble a gardener,
A wanderer,
Itself and someone else,
To roast fish on a spit for friends
To rise to heaven and be seated on the right hand of God
As befits the son.

I

Lying on that table
I hear the faint sound of a vacuum cleaner
I feel the breeze on the far edge of my body.

And everything that was in me stands tall like an army
On the very border with air
As if we could still begin a war, and lose it again.

Quick, and then slow
Like a clever dog, first it tilts its head
Then it understands, and it runs to you

So the soul probes its own housing
Curls up inside, the lining of crumbling faded velvet,
Or strokes its leathery lid.

Under the black-and-blue clouds, baroque-sombre
You are reconstituted
Like fish on a fishmonger's slab,

Your bones, your muscles – picked apart
By a doctor's prized thumbs
And there you lie, dumb.

– translated by **Sasha Dugdale**

Maurice Riordan

GRAVEL

for Frank

I, too, will spend an hour playing with the gravel.
Sorting and cleaning it. It does love the dirt.
Dead leaves, grit, seeds that can sprout. And it hides
the odd slug or worm. We can't be having that!
Some of these stones have come a great distance.

I can no longer tell which are from Uist or Orkney.
And there's one came from a mountain in Sarawak.
Could it be this basalt with the twinkle of schist?
A shame. It's somehow joined the rabble tipped
here one morning from the Travis Perkins lorry.

I'm acting the snob! Each and every anonymous stone
has its captive soul, its own fixed little being.
And stones are time travellers. They start out in lake or esker,
or on the seafloor having housed small creatures.
The very tips of the Himalayas are limestone.

All these mute souls, who can tell their journeys ...
How can I be their god! I'm too bald to be a saviour.
Though for an hour we'll sift them through our hands.
Each one – like the last poems of Celan – born dark.
Each one condemned for the duration of the earth.

Maurice Riordan

MOULD

> *Nature in the biological realm has a tendency to be fanciful*
> – Freeman Dyson

The mould on this six-week-old tomato sauce
has grown a green merino fleece with glints
of blue and orpiment and – now I blow over it –
a sheen of luminescence like an uncut hayfield.

I hesitate before ditching it, as I would a goldfish.
Or the drooping cactus. This isn't just food gone bad
but an organism with (I think) genes and enzymes.
Far beyond the chemistry of rot or ferment.

It quadrupled while we were off over-exposing
our pink skins. Jumping from the dock, whooping it up
round the barbecue, loving each other, then rowing
over loos and ice trays. Before hugging again.

Just about keeping the lid on the id, as our guts
settled into microbial harmony and we grew back
into the old us swearing and farting in chorus.
Gruntled swine. Among God's simpler creatures.

While here in the fridge dark something mycelial,
artful, got underway. With its own idea of culture.
Determined, while sensitive to initial conditions.
And now how unforeseen, and pretty, the outcome.

There we lay splayed on the deck, our skins maybe
experimenting with UV but young forever we were.
Here the pure carry-on. No plan or purpose. Or the plan
obscured in riddles of symmetry and equilibrium.

I blow again across the summer meadow. I take a pic.
One to post! Clickable. Squiggly, like a late Pollock …
And sort of tasty-looking, though it would kick up
a spectacular shit-storm in the jetlagged family gut.

So *nice try mate* down you go! In a swirl of rainbows
into carbolic suds and boiling water – a foul dybbuk
sputtering in the plughole for a fiery moment …
Then that rattle as you're sluiced past the U-bend.

Maurice Riordan

LUMPS

Spoiling the gravy, lumps.
In my cup *please, just the one.*
Still in bed at noon, the lump.
Check one side, then the other.
Often in the throat, a lump.

David McLoghlin

INDEPENDENT COMMISSION FOR THE LOCATION OF VICTIMS' SILENCE

When I was at Glenstal in the '80s, you liked
to boast about your brother, the Sinn Féin councillor.
And the thought emerges, like a fossil out of marl:
he knew the ones that gave the order.
Two hundred miles south of the Belfast Brigade's field
of operations, brindled cows cropping both sides of the Anglo-
Irish avenue, a brook whispering under a low bridge, electric fence
the only filament   I.E.D. glint of a trip wire   In the parlour
you were saying your mother – "ah, sure God rest her" – had
hosted the Army Council in her living room
and served digestive biscuits.
                                        As noduled fingers took the cosy
off the pot, they asked: "So what do you think, Mrs H?" Stooped,
she might nod – or, would she suggest juicier targets? You loved that
they loved her for that. Republican Matriarch,
their own personal Mother Ireland.
"Aye, they respected her – and sure, she herself a little old lady."
I imagine her going back to her rosary in the kitchen, goitred
with her sons' internment, and the long war's soiling.

My father hated the IRA so much
he was almost a Catholic Unionist. I was perverse,
half-proud of your connections – your spadework.
I thought I knew everything about you, Chaplain of the blood
of Pearse, Connolly and Slab Murphy.
But until I was 33, I didn't know you'd disappeared me
yourself, into the ground of my body   in several monastery rooms
while the whole country was sleeping

and detectives were sent out in plain clothes
and bullet proof in search of the Border Fox
Uzis and handsomeness at check points in West Limerick.
You were a rogue cell, condoned by the others, who nodded
as they passed us with their psalters and eyes' omertà.
There is no taut white archaeological string to mark the pit.
We know that it happened, and we know that they did it,
but not everyone has been recovered.

Emily Middleton

MISLOADED

One year before I died, you said that some bodies
are buried in the wrong graves.

It's rare now, you said, more common in the past –
in times of paper records, in times of war.

★

We never expected minds could be misfiled – how
something automated could be confused

like a clerical error. Then seven months
before I died they said everything was running

off spreadsheets. Imagine every test a fabric square,
roughly hewn, stuck, sewn – the gaps patched.

★

Five weeks before I died, I started *War and Peace*.
When you said goodbye, you found it open-mouthed

on my bedside table, two and three-quarter
chapters from the end. My watch –

the grandfather kind, you always teased –
still ticking behind a half-drunk tumbler

of institutional orange squash. The news flickering
above my bed in endless loops of red and white.

★

One year after I died, your phone pings: *On this day.*
A smiling face of a father you'd never known, an anniversary

you'd never celebrated, a garden party you'd never seen.
Instead, you think of the starched pillow,

the peeling wall facing my feet. The book, not knowing
the ending. Memories spliced, the photostream,

the gluttonous email archive, me misfiled,
under the right stone but cached in the wrong cloud.

Verified but unchecked. And after all that cash!
Curse that app, its bloated promises.

*

I imagine your mind powering up, angry,
hurtling to retrieve me – grainy me, low-res,

wearing the wrong colour jumper on your somethingth birthday
with an indeterminate fuzz of guests.

My voice perhaps a note too low but just
as sonorous: telling the same stories

for the millionth time, the one about the war,
the one about the coder, the one, the one.

Bryony Littlefair

TYPO

How am I meant to bear this, I thought, along
with everyone – the year a typo in a hyperlink –

wearing a fur coat to the funeral
like I had to become an animal to endure it.

But yesterday I woke, cheeks dry for the first time
– we'd slept for eleven hours or more –
and I said, half-dreaming,
                                        I've always
thought lesser-spotted *meant an animal*
has fewer spots and I realised just now
it means less often seen.

Maybe sometimes a strangeness arrives
and lets us free, like loving your partner afresh

when both of you are on separate walks,
and you bump into each other on the high street.

Or a thought occurring to you years after
someone's death: *they didn't do that to be mean,*
they did it because they loved me –

sounding out like a windchime across
an overgrown garden.

                        It's like the door
being on the latch when the whole time
you thought it was locked. Someone thinks
I can't bear it, and then dies. Typo.
Someone thinks *I can't bear it*, and then does.

Dane Holt

THE SKY A TOOTHACHE SHADE OF WHITE

Building the Ice Hotel hardly seems worth it.
In the foyer, clear/opaque *damier*-patterned tiles
balance grandeur and its synonyms perfectly.
Distinguished sculptures weep their tangled beards.

We tortured Mr Incumbent by entering the anteroom
with purpose only to forget what we'd come in for.
He looked up from his ottoman with a face like currency
won and lost all night across a deal table.

The campaign was not without a certain *brio*.
Those in the valley stayed put, convinced our dams
were what ancient engineers dreamed possible.
When the fighter jets made a break for it

through the thick clouds of volcanic ash, we knew time
was a factor among factors. "Friends,
once the wounds have healed we shall reflect:
collate our good deeds and our bad and these

shall form our mountain ranges, our tragic skyline.
The floods shall irrigate our tennis courts, by God!"
A drop of water runs down a seam in the Ice Cathedral dome
like word coming down the mountain any day now.

Michael Longley

WINTER SOLSTICE

i

Christmas Eve: you turn eighty today, love,
Separated by the virus from children
And grandchildren, my elderly bride asleep
Beside me at the winter solstice, days
Growing longer, the family returning,
At the bedroom window budding catkins,
House sparrows in the pink-flowered hawthorn.

ii

Now David reports from Carrigskeewaun
Choughs calling above the cottage – *pshaw pshaw* –
On their way to the Claggan roosting-cliff;
And sets free in my imagination
The swans you counted in your nightdress once
Long ago at dawn when we were lovers –
Twenty whoopers fading into snowlight.

Michael Longley

ASHES

They arrive in a little box,
My twin Peter and his widow
Quarantined outside in the porch
Until I bring into the warmth
Their mingled ashes, a portion,
The rest afloat on the North Sea.

I shall drive them to Drumbo Church
And lay them in our parents' grave
With its view across the valley
To Belfast Lough and the shipyard
Where my twin was an apprentice,
The marine engineer to be.

In the shadow of the round tower
I shall be his best man again.

Kris Johnson

THE DOE

i

Five minutes into my run,
I come across the doe.

She doesn't struggle as I slide
down the bank to kneel

beside her in the blackberry
and last autumn's alder.

I stroke her white muzzle and neck.
There, there. There, there.

As morning drones and the sun
begins to lift the frost, I rise –

stagger home on feet numbed
and blunt as hooves.

I try to wash her from me,
but the steam of her swift breathing

fills the bathroom. I wear her scent
on my wrists, the touch of fur a secret.

ii

Because once I swerved
to miss a buck on this road,
the doe is on my mind
as we slow to greet tail-lights
and a shower of glass
across the highway.

Diners from the café shiver
on the kerb, the chef
conducts traffic, and a man

with a face of stone
looms over the body
of a motorcyclist.
How small it seems
as they pull
a Pendleton blanket
head to toe.

I know the radio plays,
know sirens blare
as we let police cars pass,
but the only sound I hear
is my voice: how I tried

to comfort her
the way I remembered
and wanted my mother's touch.
I hear me tell you
of her animal warmth,
how I longed to lay beside her
the way I used to press against you
in the minutes before sleep.

Jane Draycott

THE KINGDOM

I was hungry
    coming up from Kent
after the summer resortyng hyther

my tent a riverbed
    seeking herbergement
some accommodation among the stone

the men coming on to you
    the taxi drivers saying here jump in no
no you don't need no money.

I was thirsty
    languissyng in the doorway
behind the post office

the churchyard water
    so cold for washing
and from my mouth came leaves

– what eyleth the woman? –
    and from the cracks in the pavement
came syllables.

I was a stranger
    turned half to stone seeking releyf
in severe weather

in search of something
    oute of thys madnesse
something to inherit.

Jane Draycott

OUR TOWN AND THE FALCON

Ours is roomy country, and not
just from the air –
                        down here in town
we've got several streets each
to ourselves.
            I like to walk
the place at dawn, as if I were
the only person left on the planet –

our resurfaced car park OUT ONLY,
our new public toilets built
to resemble a small alpine chalet

our hangars and halls
cleared now but for the leftover rolls
of razor wire. Authorized arrivals
only. Lots of room
            for the individual.

We have emptied our hearts
and minds. Feelings rush
towards us from the vacant sky,
bits of asteroid
            rush towards us

homing in like a falcon bringing
fresh new evidence of how
                        this could all have begun.

We are preparing to meet
that incoming space dust in every
possible way we can think of.

Jess Thayil

THE WEIGHT

~~at sixteen   beneath a stranger~~   ~~his beedi~~
~~glowing between~~ his arrack-lips   you wait for ~~light~~
burn   ~~your screams curling into the night;~~
trees transfixed above you ~~bless the fear~~ – eddy
of years to come – ~~not a witness in sight;~~
~~at sixteen~~ beneath a stranger ~~his beedi~~
~~glowing between his arrack-lips~~   you wait ~~for light~~
so ready for a girlhood to be washed away
~~by the rude rush of a man's want;~~ a burst of thunder ~~& fight~~
in this summer's sudden weeping   ~~your kick & bite~~
~~at sixteen beneath a stranger   his beedi~~
when his hands fly between ~~your throat & T Shirt~~ muddy
bra & panties   ~~printed & printed~~ blue & white;
~~at sixteen   beneath a stranger~~ his beedi
glows ~~between his arrack-lips   you wait for light~~
& printed you think ~~you are finished~~   *steady*
there! ~~but his endeavour's disrupted~~   when the sick
fountains out of your mouth;   ~~a fright~~ frozen
for the years ~~at sixteen beneath a stranger~~ – his beedi's
glow   then his beedi snuffed out   & the weight ~~of light~~

Aoife Riach

MEET ME IN THE CHARITY SHOP

Step in and let me upcycle the truth.
We'll dine in a sea of living-room sets
and musty couches for miles and miles.
I'll hand you a wine glass, tinged pink
and clunky, mine is a gold-rimmed
flute and chipped, let's toast our home,
ours and sprawling, spark up a bulb
in a moth-eaten shade, set a record
spinning, a real rare find, a turntable,
two speakers, a collector's cabinet.

Find me a dress once worn to a wedding,
threadbare and cried-in to pinch
at the hips, chase me through cast-offs,
archaic contraptions, raise dust
from our books and our chairs in our vast
dominion of mould, we're moth-food too.
For your birthday I'll give you a Millennium
Candle, zeros spiralling like frenzied icing.
Everything here meant something once,
someone died for our mildewed treasures
and you love a bargain so be smug I am
just like new I am in such good condition

John McAuliffe

SOUTERRAIN

> *i.m. Derek Mahon*

To wait things out, underground,
laid in with more than a lifetime's treasure;
to settle down with the books and study
what comes along the line.

I understand. This
must be around the turn of a millennium.
Hidden, the mind will return
to a 'proper dark'

freed from daylit distraction
to ponder absolutes
and the tenses of its own
cavernous, echoing interiors,

seeing the issue
of the day from an ancient prospect.
But terrors shake
this long night,

the texts losing their place,
soft tissue
between some future and the past perfect,
the pooled floor

rising towards the leaking roof,
which gets thundered over.
Powerful sounds scatter the animals
and the shears rust in an outhouse

while the motorway is lowered
further into the royal hill.
There are other sore spots;
a pilot light

going out at the sun's titanic western edge;
a reddening field
parched by the wind;
the myrtle and olive

grow across frivolous libraries,
their flocks gone
to pastures new
who would still graze

on these flattened fields,
their reasonable ground. Imagine
going, knowing that what you bury
promises discovery,

cropping up
like braille for the finger to trace,
making out the pattern
by when it comes to a stop

Audrey Molloy

LIFTING OFF

In 2015, when I'd been writing poems for a couple of years, I gathered them together and had twenty copies printed as a pamphlet. It was called *Hardwired*. I even had a cover designed on Fiverr – a circuit board with each wire terminating in a tiny heart. There were eighteen poems in all, including two haiku. The opener had the word 'soul' not only in the title, but twice in the poem itself, and it appeared a further nine times in the pamphlet. And there were worse crimes than that (as well as the odd decent line that has survived).

When I'm being fanciful, I think of my poetry files in metaphors: like a block of marble I chip away at, in (vain) search of the angel. Or a bonsai tree – surely the perfect metaphor for the genre? Like sculpture, the art of bonsai lies in the choice of what to keep – a twist here, a loose strand there – and what to remove.

But the metaphor I most often return to is the idea of a poet's work as a kind of rocket ship, navigating the challenges of lift-off and bucking gravity in its trajectory through the atmosphere. Various stages fall away – some salvaged for parts, others left to sink beneath the sea. Only the capsule completes the journey into orbit, where it can stay in a holding pattern indefinitely, or negotiate blunt-body re-entry after some time.

One of the biggest challenges I faced when navigating my journey to publication was my identity as a writer. Even as a child I had a foot in both my native Dublin and the rural Wexford of my formative years. For the past two decades I've been an Irish woman in Sydney, with both countries duelling for my heart. During a poetry workshop several years ago, an established Australian poet asked me if I was an Irish or Australian poet. His question baffled me. Surely a poem was a poem and could be conceived and written (and enjoyed) on any continent? He didn't agree. A poet is connected to place, he said. I didn't believe him for years. But where to publish was a question I wrestled with. I figured I could do live readings (ha! Remember those?) in Australia to promote a book, but could I write authentically about eucalypts and creeks when sycamores and wild coastlines were what I knew best?

I continued to write. *Hardwired* evolved into *Fault Lines* and then became *Mother Creature*, and so on. Some versions had mocked-up cover designs. For years I sent them far and wide, editing, reformatting, and re-titling relentlessly. Occasionally, one would make a shortlist. On my third or fourth attempt at the Munster Literature Centre's Fool for Poetry competition, my pamphlet *Satyress* was selected as runner-up, and was published by Southword Editions in 2020.

Somewhere around this time the answer to that question I'd baulked at years before came to me: though I lived in Sydney, I was an Irish writer. Some poems I'd had published in various journals (including this one) came to the attention of Peter Fallon, editor of The Gallery Press. He enquired if I had a book to send him. If I'd had to start putting a collection together at that point, I doubt I could have done so. But there had been all those mock-ups. Turns out I'd been in the simulator for years.

I sent off my book-length manuscript a couple of weeks after Peter got in touch. He liked it. And it felt right to me too. But that was by no means the final book. Stages of the ship continued to fall away for several months: notions of title, cover design, order of contents, and many poems (one third of what I'd sent, some jettisoned willingly, others requiring a hard swallow), and all under the guidance of the endlessly patient team at Gallery.

Of the twenty poems in my pamphlet, *Satyress*, poems that I believed only a year ago represented my best work, only nine appear in *The Important Things*. And there's even one in there from *Hardwired*, barely edited from the original.

In order for a spaceship to launch, the anchoring bolts must explode. One of these bolts is the inner censor. The realisation that I am not writing for my parents, children, exes, in-laws, teachers, school-friends, or parish priests is liberating. Unless they are poets themselves, or people who buy and read books by poets they haven't met, they are not my audience. Like most of the poems that are written in a lifetime, that censor has to be abandoned. Only when that final bolt blows away is the rocket ship ready for lift off.

Philip Coleman

AWING ALL

Paula Meehan, *As If By Magic: Selected Poems* (Dedalus Press, 2020), €18.
Sinéad Morrissey, *Found Architecture: Selected Poems* (Carcanet Press, 2020),
£14.99.

In an essay called 'Magic' published in 1901, WB Yeats began with the
following declaration:

> I believe in the practice and philosophy of what we have agreed to
> call magic, in what I must call the evocation of spirits, though I do not
> know what they are, in the power of creating magical illusions, in the
> visions of truth in the depths of the mind when the eyes are closed ...

Many would scoff today, as they probably did in his time, at Yeats's belief
in the esoteric. However, if we allow for an understanding of poetry
that accepts the idea that 'vision' is central to its pursuit of truth, then it
is hard to escape Yeats's formulation. We may wish to ignore or deny it
altogether – Yeats himself often wished to put 'this belief in magic from
[him] if [he] could' – but a century and more of analytic philosophy and
various forms of formalist criticism have not destroyed the desire to use
poetry, and other forms of art, as a way to create 'magical illusions'.
Critical schools such as the New Criticism may have fostered a new
appreciation of formal analysis in literary interpretation in the last century,
but for poets – and readers, especially those outside the academy –
Yeats's belief in 'what we have agreed to call magic', however we define
it, is a central part of the experience of writing, and reading, poetry.

The works of several contemporary Irish poets come to mind in this
context, from Brendan Kennelly's *A Man Made of Rain* to Máighréad
Medbh's *Parvit of Agelast*. It is relevant too in relation to Paula Meehan
and Sinéad Morrissey, two poets who have between them published
several books that have helped to extend the boundaries of Irish poetry in
the last quarter-century by being willing to explore the magical
possibilities of the form. Shunning a poetry of mere description – personal
or social – while at the same time writing poems that are often unapolo-
getically physical in their bodily and political rootedness, they have both
insisted on an appreciation of what Morrissey terms those 'theophanies /
that awed all Anatolia, / / upon which our modernday / buoyancy
depends', in her magnificent poem 'The Book of Knowledge of Ingenious
Mechanical Devices'. 'Flick open his pages', she writes:

and listen to the clicking

of dismantled
humanoid automata
reconstructing themselves

from the bottom
up, then stepping back
from the task accomplished

Although she is referring here to the author of the ninth-century work
upon which the poem is based, reading Morrissey's poems – and the
same point holds for Meehan – we encounter living souls on every page
that are brought to life by these poets' masterful, magical, handling of
form and language.

In 'The Solace of Artemis' (2015), the second of her lectures as holder
of the Ireland Chair of Poetry between 2013 and 2016, Paula Meehan
acknowledges the 'power of memory, of language' to 'reach back' into
experience, in this case 'to console [a] child with ... burned hands, to tell
her nothing is ever lost that has made its way into poetry.' Meehan's
lectures record her personal and professional journey as a poet in intimate and informative ways, from her experiences growing up in Dublin
in the 1950s and '60s to studying with scholars and poets such as WB
Stanford, Gary Snyder, and James J McAuley later on. Meehan's lectures
reveal so much about her emergence as an Irish poet of unique and
distinctive gifts since the 1980s, but they return again and again to
acknowledge the mystical and magical sources of her art. In her lecture
'Planet Water' (2016), she compares reading the I Ching to the process of
reading poems, while in 'The Solace of Artemis' she writes: 'Whatever
is held in the myths [including the story of Artemis] […] resonates in the
living body, the way a poem might use the human body, in the ritual
re-enactment of the breath from which it is made, to re-experience itself.'
Meehan seems to describe this process in a poem called 'The Hexagram'
from her 2016 collection *Geomantic*, which is included in her *Selected Poems*:

Before starting find the lines – broken
and whole – arranged as a hexagram;
the crescent moon waxing, a token

in the night sky of beginnings. Palms
open to the grace of what might fall
like snow to the snow-white page. How calm

I am, and cool, when I hear the call.
She has found me out, in my silence,
come with rumours of heaven, of hell.

This is a remarkable poem of poetic creation and discovery – of the poet coming into being in the process of being discovered by the goddess, Artemis, to whom so many of Meehan's poems pay homage. As she puts it in the first piece ('Before the Pubs Close') in the triptych 'Three Paintings of York Street' from *The Man Who Was Marked By Winter* (1991): 'Quick. Before the moon is eaten / by that cloud, rescue its dust ...'

The world of Meehan's poems is suffused with moonlight: a poem comes 'to light / / through the pulse beating / wane of the moon' in 'Tanka', from *Painting Rain* (2009), while in 'Death of a Field' from the same collection she describes a field before it has 'become map memory / In some archive on some architect's screen' in 'its moon white caul'. These images are not esoteric, however, and it is important to stress that Meehan's lunar obsessions are not otherworldly. On the contrary, they represent the poet's deep connectedness to things, her sense of the interrelationships between self and world and – as a woman – her lifelong record of the rhythms of the universe as they pervade her own living, singing soul. 'I'm an ordinary woman / tied to the moon's phases', she writes in 'Not Your Muse' from *Pillow Talk* (1994), but the sky from which the light of Artemis shines is often 'brutal' and 'merciless'. In this regard, Meehan is the author of some of the most powerful poems about sexual violence and loss ever written by an Irish poet, from her early poems 'Elegy for a Child', 'Child Burial', and 'The Statue of the Virgin at Granard Speaks' in *The Man Who Was Marked By Winter*, to a middle-aged mother being taught 'the new facts of life' in 'Troika' from *Painting Rain*.

Meehan's poems are written under many lunar signs: 'Moons like petals adrift on the stream', as she puts it in 'The Moons' from *Geomantic*. *As If By Magic*, her selected poems up to and including that collection, is a powerful testament to a true original in Irish poetry, a poet whose voice and vision are unmistakable and important for what she has to say as much as how she says it. Constantly exploring and crafting new forms – *Geomantic* is also significant in this regard – Meehan is unafraid to risk personal exposure or hold back socio-political comment. The directness of her language gives way to a depth of insight that places her among a visionary company that includes Yeats and William Blake. Words she writes for her grandmother in 'St. John and my Grandmother – an Ode' from *Painting Rain* are appropriate, too, for Meehan herself:

Avatar of hearth mysteries,
true daughter of the moon, the shining one,
before she'd open the curtains of morning

whether winter or summer while the kettle boiled
she'd tell her dreams to her gathered daughters,
as apocalyptic in their cast as were St. John's.

Remembering her grandmother, Meehan says that it was her 'dream tongue' that provided her 'first access to poetry'; her poems have their source in her grandmother's 'dream songs for her daughters'. Between 'Mary McCarthy and the Evangelist John' – the poet's grandmother and the author of the Book of Revelation (with a nod, too, to John Berryman) – *As If By Magic* confirms Meehan's place not only as a great Irish poet but as a writer whose work should resonate with readers of poetry wherever it is read and appreciated.

Sinéad Morrissey shares many things with Paula Meehan. They are both poets of cities (Belfast and Dublin respectively), but also of international travel – between them their work ranges from Greece to China, New Zealand, and many points between. However, they are also both poets of home and they write movingly of love, relationships, family, and loss in all of their personal and cultural reverberations. In Morrissey's poem 'Zero', from *The State of the Prisons* (2005), she describes the intricate relations that bind objects and concepts while at the same time revealing the often costly and painful human dramas that underlie historical events and discoveries. There is something playful about this poem but, like all play, the message is serious, as it is in the games played by children in 'The Rope', from *On Balance* (2017), where the poet sees a symbol of 'sibling-tetheredness, an umbilicus' in the 'flotsam of props' her children have put out on her 'tarmacked driveway'.

Morrissey has an incredible eye for detail and she always seems to find just the right formal arrangement to capture the things she is describing: 'Colour Photographs of Tsarist Russia' is a striking example of this, also from *On Balance*. At the same time, however, and like Meehan, Morrissey is not afraid to press beyond the surfaces of things, to go beyond 'a crack in the pattern's / typography', as she writes in the poem that gives her selected poems its title, 'Found Architecture', from *Through the Square Window* (2009). Recalling the arrival of a gift – an 'Italian kaleidoscope' – she describes how:

The day it arrived I mangled the blue of the bathroom
with the pistachio green of my bedroom ceiling

and sat entranced: such symmetrical splicing
of everything, anything, to make my waiting-house
a star-pointed frame that entered and left

itself behind as the cylinder turned. Any light that there was
was instantly mystical – a crack in the pattern's
typography, like the door at the end of the corridor

shedding radiance.

Towards the end of this poem, Morrissey writes of how, 'From blood
and the body's / inconsolable hunger I have been my own kaleidoscope'.
This is an unforgettable image of the self that affirms both the physical
and the aesthetic aspects of loss and experience as they are mediated and
intertwined in the mind of the poet.

Morrissey's poems radiate different kinds of energy – physical,
emotional, intellectual – and she records and acknowledges a multiform
universe, one that cannot be explained away by science but for which
we also require the visionary insights of poetry. Her poem 'Matter',
also from *Through the Square Window*, makes this argument succinctly:
Aristotle may have 'observed and recorded it all' but witches still 'con-
sulted the sky' long after him, and still do so today. 'And though I know',
she writes, 'thanks in part to Pasteur', how her child came to be:

> I still think
> of our lovemaking as a kind of door
> to wherever you were, waiting in matter,
> spooled into a form I have not yet been shown
> by the unprompted action of nature ...

Throughout her poems, Morrissey reveals things that are often hidden
from plain sight, even in our most intimate relationships with others.
Her poems give form, indeed, to those things that, for most of us, remain
formless until they have been articulated by a poet of her great gifts.

Beginning with *There Was Fire in Vancouver* (1996), Morrissey has gone
from strength to strength as a poet, not just in terms of her formal com-
mand, but also in terms of conceptual and intellectual richness and reach.
She is always probing beyond the immediately perceptible into the next
dimension, wherever that may take her, as she shows in 'The Singing
Gates' from *On Balance*. 'I want to ask you about the gates' the speaker
says, and about 'this particular calibre of sound / unravelling only here'.
In Morrissey's poems, the mysteries of people and places and things are
unravelled in ways that are truly remarkable to read, line by line, poem
by poem, collection by collection. The publication of *Found Architecture:
Selected Poems* is a tremendous mid-career affirmation and achievement.

Nidhi Zak/Aria Eipe

SIXTEEN STEPS TOWARDS A FIRST COLLECTION: A THREAD

> An arrow shot by an archer, a poem made by a poet
> should cut through your heart, jolting the head.
> If it doesn't – it's no arrow, it's no poem.
>   – Nanne Choda, 12th century CE

Putting together a first book is like a lot of firsts in life – everyone seems to have an opinion yet, when you get to it, you struggle to recall any advice. Much of it you won't (need to) remember; some of it will twig long after and you'll go, Ah! that's what they were on about.

First collections can often start out having a wide-ranging scope. It's tempting to include every brilliant poem you've ever written. But a collection of poems is different to a Collected Poems. A collection is similar to a bow: it needs to have a spine before you can string it.

Listen for the pulse of your poems. What is it that you want to make manifest – not simply with *a book* of poems, but with *this book*? Marina Tsvetaeva's injunction is worth returning to: 'One should write only those books from whose absence one suffers.'

Think about what your book might bring to the world – a new slant, an angle, a mode of seeing – that hasn't been explored in that way before. Because if it does this for you, it's almost guaranteed it will do it for someone else, then another, and another.

A key element of a collection is structure. A collection charts a journey, a relationship with time. Some transformation must occur over the course of the journey, whether this is evident in the narrative arc or marks a more subtle, inner change in the writer or reader.

It can be difficult to figure this out on your own, so share your work with people – other writers, readers, poets – whose instincts you trust. Ask them what they see. Others tend to be more articulate about, and – often – so much kinder to your work than you might ever be.

They'll also notice where you use the word 'dark' or 'bone' across four different poems, where you end two subsequent poems with a falling bird, or say helpful things like: "It seems that flight is really integral to your work", which you can then confidently use in your pitch.

Choose sample poems with an eye to showcasing the range of your writing. Editors will frequently receive portfolios where the poems are very similar in tone, style, or form. A compelling collection is varied and surprising. Play your strongest hand.

It's easier to find a publisher than it is to find *your* publisher. Spend time researching the ethos and values of potential presses and publishing houses. It's an important relationship: you both have to be able to find pleasure in it, grow together, and want to stay in it.

Don't write yourself off. If you've given it everything, shoot for the moon! Make a ranked list of where you want to submit and send out in order of your dream presses. Most poetry publishers welcome unagented submissions, and many will advertise an annual open submissions window.

Look up publishers' websites and follow their guidelines. If they request ten pages of poetry, don't send twenty. If they don't ask to see your CV, don't send one. If they are old school and want printed copies through the post, mail a nice handwritten note along with the poems.

Send some poems from your manuscript to literary journals or magazines. It lets you see what editors are drawn to, where your strengths lie, which areas need more work. It also helps in navigating the process of submissions, and doggedly holding out hope in the face of rejection.

Sometimes, an editor might decline your work but also send feedback – this is gold. Use it to enhance future submissions. It helps to start – or focus on – some other creative project while you wait, letting you gain distance from, and perspective on, the work you've sent out.

Scour the acknowledgements pages of collections you admire and look into how to link up with some of the people or organisations mentioned there, through courses, workshops, or even informally. Being part of a generous, honest, supportive community is one of the perks of poetry.

All this can seem daunting, and occasionally is, but it's also a wild, magical trip. You only get to do it once, so go all out: in ways that lift your spirit, with people who believe in you. Trust that your work is vital and necessary. Yours is a voice; it's one we need to hear.

Grace Wilentz

OF PAMPHLETS AND POLITICS

Joe Carrick-Varty, *54 questions for the man who sold a shotgun to my father* (Out-Spoken Press, 2020), £7.
Audrey Molloy, *Satyress* (Southword Editions, 2020), €6.
Breda Spaight, *The Untimely Death of My Mother's Hens* (Southword Editions, 2019), €6.
Mícheál McCann, *Safe Home* (Green Bottle Press, 2020), £6.
Mark Ward, *Carcass* (Seven Kitchens Press, 2020), $9.
Eva Griffin, *Fake Hands, Real Flowers* (Broken Sleep Books, 2019), £6.50.

When I first told my friends in the US that I was publishing a pamphlet, they assumed it was some sort of political manifesto. It's true, the political pamphlet was once an important medium for the spread of ideas, and yet these six contemporary poetry pamphlets are too. Some deal with political issues head on, while others do so more subtly and through the lens of the personal. But what is most interesting to me about all these new offerings is the different ways they conceive of what it is to be human, alive, and inside of a body in the context of a state whose laws can seemingly offer both freedom and protection, yet so often fail to do so.

54 questions for the man who sold a shotgun to my father is Joe Carrick-Varty's second pamphlet. The central concern here is permanent separation, but indirectly the work also points to an unbroken connectedness between people and events. 'And God said' is a meditation on causation, hinting at the underlying unity of the world through which every action has an equal and opposite reaction. Events which appear unrelated are brought into a choreography of immediacy:

> Every time a whale is born albino
> a man doesn't die of liver failure and every time
> it rains at sea a child speaks first words.

The narrative thread in *54 questions* builds towards 'THE CHILDREN', a poem in which the act of a father's suicide transforms his children's lives forever. The title poem peppers childlike questions with more ominous ones that ultimately throw into stark relief the laxity of gun laws, the societies that give rise to them, and the ordinariness of all of us who participate in the status quo:

> Did he tell you what he wanted it for / Did you ask / Did he smile /
> Did you touch / Talk much/ Had he shaved / If you could use a

number to describe his laugh would you use 1000 or 3 / Did you
put the money towards a loft extension / Is that a lasagne in your
oven?

54 questions is powerful and effective in marrying the personal and the
political. Though it contains only twelve poems, this pamphlet achieves
significant breadth and emotional depth.

Audrey Molloy is an Irish poet based in Sydney. Her pamplet, *Satyress*,
opens with an enigmatic epigraph that sets up this intuitive and resonant
debut:

> We call it *the body* but see one skin—
> furred or bare—and a glimpse of pink whale
> behind ivory teeth; a keratin sheet,
> two holes to look in.

These poems have a refreshing diversity of form. 'Still Sequence: The
Last Year' counts the months, marking them with snapshots that
approach encapsulation, but are at the same time diaristic. They lead us
towards the central concern of *Satyress*, the end of a marriage and
relocating one's sense of self:

> *Oct*
> A child freewheeling downhill with legs outstretched,
>   finding her balance.
>
> *Nov*
> A park bench where a woman shares the same moon as her lover
>   on the other side of the harbour.
>
> *Dec*
> A silver tree decoration on a fine, white ribbon, reflecting a family
>   for one last time.

The voice at the heart of these poems moves between inhabiting her life,
standing outside it, sliding into fantasy, all with a wink and a sense of
humour. The figure of the satyress stalks these poems, in which the voice
revels in perspectival slippage and in surreal experiences of the familiar,
as in 'Double-Life Diary':

> Afterwards. She puzzles her reflection, cloven
> by the make-up mirror: twelve selves

refracted from the bevel, yet she can live
only two lives, in a strange, marled existence.

Audrey Molloy's *Satyress* is intelligent, fun, and moving, an elegant debut signalling exciting things to come.

Breda Spaight's first pamphlet, *The Untimely Death of My Mother's Hens*, presents six stand-alone poems followed by 'Amongst Men', a series of fifteen unnumbered sonnets with a linked narrative thread. Spaight's scientific eye for detail is part of what makes this work so unflinching. In the title poem, the image of the disposal of dead birds borders somewhere between clinical and humorous, before the undercurrent of grief hits a nerve:

It is easy to deal with the dead

ones – rigid, puffed bodies. I fork one
then another into the bushes. The living

stagger in the daylight. They coo
like a mother's lullaby; feathers fanned

frozen in the act of ruffling.

These poems remind us that we are somatic creatures, living in bodies, surviving and making sense of experiences that are often complex and conflicting. This deepens and darkens in 'Amongst Men', the pamphlet's second half, where the recurring figures of a man and a woman evolve through intimacy, desire, violence, and control.

Coal shovel on the table: last night's beating.
She clasps her fingers around her stomach.
There, there, she says; feels it kick.
Its first kick followed the first blow.
She'd held her stomach like you'd run
with washing from the line when rain comes,
the spit of his words on her face –
It isn't fucking mine.

Spaight's debut pamphlet is not for the faint-hearted: one reviewer noted it for being 'visceral'. But this pamphlet is timely. In the context of Covid-19, we know more than ever that violence in the home was and is the experience of many, particularly of women. Why then should we look away? I came away from *The Untimely Death of My Mother's Hens* asking myself productive questions, such as, What can occupy the poem? And, For what reasons do we read?

Mícheál McCann's debut pamphlet, *Safe Home*, is permeated by a sense of purity; his poems have a way of holding space for themselves. McCann explores themes of home, growing up, sexuality, friendship, and family. His awareness of inequality is a persistent preoccupation throughout. In 'Peadar's', the experience of a pub-wide sing-along of 'Fairytale of New York' is felt acutely:

> Everyone cheers when *Fairytale* starts.
>
> Even the bartenders stop. Teeth full of milk.
> There are more teeth, more smiles than ways
>
> to feasibly escape.

And yet, experiences of exclusion or rejection are balanced with a sense of belonging, as in 'Leaving London for Belfast', where McCann writes:

> My tired thighs hear
> where we're going over the tannoy
> and I can hear Jo Stafford
> smiling as she sings. I missed you.
> I hoak for a life vest under my seat
> to realise I was wearing it all along.

McCann largely seems to be writing about his own experience, which lends *Safe Home* a gentle authority and authenticity. *Safe Home* is also deeply reflective; friendships and caring are lovingly savoured in this thoughtful and understated debut.

Mark Ward is the founding editor of *Impossible Archetype*, an international journal of LGBTQ+ poetry, now in its fourth year. *Carcass* is his second chapbook. Entering its world of flesh and disintegration, what strikes the reader first is the performative quality of the poems. They seem to want to come off the page. This is not entirely surprising as, in addition to wearing the hats of poet and editor, Ward is also a cabaret performer. In 'The Swamp', Ward begins by imaginatively constructing a literal set on which the poem will play out:

> The place itself primordial,
> some Beckett set design:
> a mound to rest against
> surrounded by darkness,
> charcoal underfoot.

One of the most startling poems in the collection, 'Blue Boy' is a kind of extended monologue in which the speaker enacts a ghastly and lethal revenge on a homophobic flatmate. The poem, with its unusual but assured rhythm, seems written for the stage:

> Have I regrets? I have plenty. Would I have done things differently?
> Probably. Does your mother miss you? I imagine so. Is the world
> better without you? I know so. Will an audience member here
> tonight report me? Possibly. And I would go quietly. And I would go
> quietly. And if they don't, what will you do?

Carcass is gritty and raw, with elements of horror. It's a pamphlet that wants to directly engage with its reader in order to elicit a strong reaction, and pulls out all the stops to do so.

Eva Griffin's *Fake Hands, Real Flowers* has a logic all its own. The poems range in location from Dublin to New York, but seem to be most at home when examining – and shattering – gender roles. At times, the pamphlet reads like a catalogue of all of the ways in which one can be bad at being female – too desperate, too sad, not wifely enough, too much like one's mother. There's humour and intelligence in how the figures in these pages resist definition as pin-ups, or saints, and insist on their own and each other's humanity, as in 'Frances, I love you':

> Frances, I'll call you
> Frances and tell you that your real name is
> beautiful, but I love you
> As Carole and I love you bleached, nervous, swinging
> a hoop from your hips and singing, I love you pinned-up
> and dumped, B-rolled and rallying, even childless, even
> selling me cheesecake.

This poem and others form part of a series exploring the relationship between actress Carole Landis and Jacqueline Susann, author of *Valley of the Dolls*. Sometimes surreal, sometimes dream-like, they work as a vehicle for something deeply felt, as in 'The Many Loves of Jackie Susann':

> At 14, Jackie looks up the word 'lesbian'
> at the library and sees a photo of herself
> as in dreams holding Molly close and dancing.

Eva Griffin's poems have a startling immediacy, and are always engrossing.

The politics of finding yourself, the politics of medicine, of protection from violence, of ending a marriage, of selling a firearm, of gender roles

– all are concerns that emerge organically in these six poetry pamphlets. They mystify and rattle and remind us that the poem is a place for freedom, and for declaring individual standards of beauty and justice. Each of these works is well worth a read. They will resource your interior life and enhance your ability to imagine what it is like to be other people. Each for less than a tenner. Lucky you.

IN CONVERSATION: THE QUEER BODY

> The following is an edited transcript of an online discussion which took place on 3/12/2020, as part of The Dublin Book Festival. The discussion, with poets Seán Hewitt, Liz Quirke, and Mark Ward, and facilitator Sasha de Buyl, began after a reading by all three poets.

Sasha de Buyl: We've thrown down the gauntlet in terms of a theme for discussion tonight, *The Queer Body*. What a fantastic theme to start with, something that is woven throughout all of your work and in very different ways, as we heard in your readings. I was hoping that you could start us off perhaps by each telling us a bit about how you reflect upon that theme in your work, and why it's important to you in your writing?

Mark Ward: *Carcass* is a strange book, it's my little book of darkness and about the dark side of the queer body. It's very much about … you see poems about S&M, there's one about a character who's a prostitute in Sofia, in Bulgaria. It's about the more dangerous side of the queer body, the pitfalls, the urges, the desires that lead to darker things, and kind of navigating that as a queer man in the modern age, mediated by cities and technology and things like that.

Seán Hewitt: My book [*Tongues of Fire*] is a book of lyric poems, so it's by definition about a queer body, that's kind of its origin point. But I think all the way through, what the book is doing – or what I think it might be doing – is looking for queer forms in the natural world and trying to make connections between different queernesses. There are a lot of things making themselves in strange ways, or growing, a lot of disregarded funguses and things like that. So, I think if anything, it's playing on the perceptions of the queer body, as in the queer body perceiving, and then perceiving the queernesses in the natural world and the interrelation between those two things. That's how I approached it.

Liz Quirke: My first collection [*The Road, Slowly*] was representative of the queer body as a site of a kinship formation, and it was very much defined by that, my poetry and that aesthetic. I was writing about the queer body as being defined by what it didn't do. I'm the non-biological mother to two smashing young daughters, and it was just that, it was family formation, considering how maternity is so defined. And then, in the second book [*How We Arrive in Winter*, forthcoming], I started look-ing at the queer body and queerness as something either responding to fracture or as hosting sites of fracture, trying to explain the inexplicable, I suppose. There's a lot more fragmentation in this one. The first book is nice and lyrical and nearly nuclear, so that was kind of a rebellion in itself, but now it's a strange amalgamation of form.

Sasha: To me, the idea of writing in an embodied state and talking about specific queernesses, especially more explicit ones, is, or at least was until recently, a fairly transgressive act. There's a lot of stuff that people didn't talk about. I liked, for example Mark, the interplay of just using a title like 'Promiscuous', to almost say, 'Well, this is what you're expecting. So, I'm just going to put it out there.' Is embodying that in your writing, and putting specific, graphic detail into your work, more important for queer writers?

Mark: I think if it's part of a story you're telling, it's important to be brave and put it all out there. It can be nerve-wracking. My first collection [*Nightlight*, forthcoming] opens with a character basically getting fucked in a sex club, so I'm aware that all the people I know are going to read this, and that's the very first poem in the first collection. So that's kind of, well, every non-poet assumes that the 'I' in poetry is you. They'll read it biographically, certainly.

Seán: My take would be that there's no imperative, or there's no *one* subject for queerness. And although I think each of our books does deal with the body, I think it's also really important to reserve a space for queer poets to do whatever else they want to do as well, and not to be defined. Not that they're not defined by their queerness, but perhaps it's a misunderstanding of queerness: any poem is kind of queered by the fact of its emerging out of a queer person, so I don't think it necessarily needs to deal with 'queer' subject matter. Also, as you said, we've had over the past couple of years an emergence of queer writing, and I think there's already the danger that it becomes seen as normal or depoliticized to say those things, because we've had our shock moment and then it's fine, it's done. So, I think there is a value in keeping shocking people into realising that it's not done, just because it's in poetry doesn't mean it's not still a thing. There can be a danger, I think, in poking your head up and then just sitting back comfortably.

Sasha: And I think that ties in nicely to what Liz was saying, during her reading – instead of having explicitly queer subject matter in your work, trying to queer the form and, for example, queering grief and queering mourning.

Liz: Yeah. It's funny, I think in the first collection, that's largely domestic and about motherhood. It's nearly nuclear iterations of family. We went through this sort of gentility phase around the marriage equality referendum, and then when you're raising two small girls in Connemara, there's a certain aspect of yourself that you do want to keep private. So, I was very protective of that essence, that body, that way of embodying the world. Whereas in the second collection, I'm a lot freer. I'm not necessarily saying that I'm going out to queer everything willy-nilly, but I'm less protective of myself and less protective of my work and what I might give away.

Sasha: I feel like that is a journey, as Seán was saying, to package up and make palatable LGBTQIA experience and communities, and marriage equality, whenever that's on the table, really does do that. It goes, 'Let's homogenize this. Let's make this really nice and tight and neat.' What I enjoyed about your collection, Liz, is that it takes that apart. It dismantles it, and says, 'These things are not as simple as they may look.'

Liz: It's all about unravelling, I think.

Sasha: I want to touch on the idea of the 'I' in poetry, as often women, and minorities, anyone who is writing from an experience that has not been as 'seen', be that in fiction, non-fiction, or poetry, will just get immediately put on hold. People always think, or just assume, that this work is highly confessional, deeply personal. I wondered if you write from a 'self' kind of 'I'? Is there a distance there? Or do you enjoy playing with that and keeping people on their toes?

Liz: There's not much distance to be honest, what you see is what you get in my work, at the moment. I'd love to do something like – the Galway poet James Martyn Joyce has a character, Furey, and there have been other concept collections, *Cailleach: The Hag of Beara* by Leanne O'Sullivan is absolutely beautiful. I'd love to have a stab at something like that at some point. But for now, I'm kind of going through the lyric 'I' for what it's worth.

Seán: Although most of the poems do come from, or are sparked by, a personal experience, they're framed in such a way as to make the 'I' almost a character of yourself. It's never you fully. And it's also you. Or, often the way I make a poem is to put one experience up against another thing and to frame it in a different way. So that distorts or electrifies, hopefully, the actual experience. I think there are levels of fictionality at play all the time, and just to remember the fact that it's a poem and we don't live inside it.

Mark: What a pity that we don't, sometimes! For me, my first book was a narrative based around a character, so it was entirely a fictional 'I', but I enjoy playing with that. Like Seán said, you can write an 'I' that's yourself and not yourself, but I absolutely enjoy writing in a variety of different voices that aren't me. Even when the poem is inspired by something in my life and I'm putting the collection together, I'm always thinking about the narrative and the 'I' as the narrator in that poem. It's not me or it's not somebody else. It's just the narrator of that piece of work.

Liz: I love distorting time. I like bringing things backwards and forwards, and then that confuses the whole thing. In the first collection, it looks like this linear narrative, but it's actually not, there are fabricated elements to it, where I've just made this sort of cutesy timeline. And then in the second collection, the one that's coming out soon, the past is very much as important as the present, and that can be quite a distortion for a reader as well. Bringing you right back to nineties Tralee and polyester track-suits, things like that.

Sasha: I very much enjoyed the polyester tracksuit, that's one for me. Mark, you mentioned writing in character and there's a piece in *Carcass* that stood out for me, which is 'Blue Boy'. I thought that was absolutely brilliant. It covers some fairly difficult themes that I honestly can't remember reading a poem about before. So, I'd love to hear a bit more about how that came to be, how you formed and shaped that piece.

Mark: Yeah, 'Blue Boy' is a twenty-minute spoken-word play that I did a number of times. I used to go to spoken-word events and go, 'Oh my god, they're amazing. I wish I could be like them.' So, I decided I would write something and of course, being me, it turned into this weird, dark thing about a man being assaulted by his roommate and wreaking revenge upon him, written in this kind of musical spoken word. I performed it at a number of theatre festivals and it was quite the experience. It is very much not myself, and I suppose with it being a theatrical thing that I staged and presented, the 'I' was even more broken down, and people were coming up and hugging me afterwards and crying. It was a very intense experience.

Sasha: Liz, you mentioned when reading that your second book is not very cheery, and it really isn't! It's a collection full of grief. Seán, I know that *Tongues of Fire* touches on loss also. I wanted to check in with both of you to ask how you approach a subject like this? How does it feel to work through painful experiences and make them manageable for a reader, to make them aesthetically pleasing, digestible? How do you break down grief like that into poetic form?

Liz: It's been an interesting process, with this second book, because I don't think I've been as conscious of its composition as I was with the first. There was a lot of painstaking craft and soul-searching with the first book, whereas in this book, a lot of the poems are hooked in a specific memory, so it's about honouring that. And I've let the form become a bit more ragged and just let things disperse across pages, in a way. The fragmentation and the physical form on the page have been freeing. I'm kind of slow to make decisions about things, so I won't really know how to define the book until maybe in five years' time.

Seán: I think we can all recognise that tendency. I can't write a poem if I ever think someone is going to read it, because if I had the reader in my head, I would freeze up, it's like being watched. I couldn't do it. I think I wrote the poems almost as if I was writing them to myself, to figure out what it was I was feeling or wanted to say. And then, equally, I have to forget that anyone's read them, in order to be happy with the fact that they're there. So, sometimes I think, like Mark said, people know more about you than you consciously think that they know, because you have to parcel yourself off, put it in a book, and say goodbye. So, yeah, for me, I mean I love my readers, but I do have to close the door on them when I'm writing.

Sasha: Seán, I wanted to ask about the work in *Tongues of Fire*. Something that I loved about it is how vividly you rendered nature, it really comes alive in language, and we the readers are placed into nature for the duration of the book. We are afforded a glimpse of the beautiful and the strange, and that's both rare and interesting – funguses that kind of sprout up from various trees ... But then also, queer encounters. I loved the placing of these subjects with equal weight in the collection, as things that you might come upon in a forest. But also, both felt like private moments made open and vulnerable, which reminded me of the fact that in the past, a lot of private, internal spaces were out of reach for queer people, and the outdoors is where things had to take place.

Seán: Well, it was important for me not to have a themed book. I wanted to have an ecosystem of themes, that would all speak to each other, and the poems might bounce and echo across each other. And so, setting them in similar places or grounding them in the natural world helped to locate them, I think, and then all those things could happen around it. With some of those poems that are confessional or that put private things on the page, I wasn't brave enough to send them out for awhile, until I sent them to a friend who liked them, and then you kind of build your confidence and make it through. And maybe it's a process that we all go through, which is getting rid of your shame. And the more you actually put it down on paper, the more you say it, the more you're like, 'Okay, well it's not that bad. It's just a poem.' The more poems you write, the braver you are. So, although they are personal things, I think as well in the context of a poem, it's like lifting the memory out, putting it on a page, and then it exists there. And you remember it, but it also lives in the poem now. There's a weird way in which it's not yours anymore, which is nice in some ways.

Mark: And let's be honest, if it gets too close, we can still turn around and say, 'Oh no, that's just a character, I'm playing with character.'

Liz: Jane Hirshfield talks about arriving at points of originality, when she arrives at a moment of risk in the poem, so it's a risk to your perception of yourself, a risk to your reputation, and all these things. I want to arrive at those points, and then whatever scary stuff happens afterwards, at least the writing has achieved what I wanted it to.

Seán: I always have that sensation that if I reach the end of a poem and it's not been uncomfortable to get there, I'm so suspicious of that poem because I don't get that moment of risk, or that moment of having to wrangle with the words or with yourself. That's what makes it work.

Sasha: I'd like to broaden the discussion out a little to talk about community context, herstory, all the things that are so important to the queer community. Firstly, I want to say that I'm genuinely delighted that there's this much queer writing in Ireland now, because as a queer person growing up in Ireland, I didn't know that any of it existed. It's lovely to see that and to see the building up of a community. I wonder if you could all speak to that a little bit. Liz, I know you're involved in the Queer Arts Collective. Mark, you run an LGBTQ+ writing journal.

Mark: I was just thinking about queer writing in Ireland, I think it definitely has grown. There's an anthology of queer writing since 2000 in the offing [*Queering the Green*, edited by Paul Maddern, forthcoming from The Lifeboat Press], which is very exciting, and that there's enough to have a big book about it is great, but I think definitely people are doing new work and putting out pamphlets and first collections. I think people are taking risks and the queer writers are leading that at the moment, they seem to be the most interesting voices. I'm perhaps biased, but definitely.

Liz: In my research, I've come across a lot of poets in maybe the last forty years who would have been queer poets, but they would have veiled their subject matter. And then you have writers like Mary Dorcey, who were explosive and activist, and were so important. It's funny now, the work that I'm doing is traversing maybe fifty odd years and a few different jurisdictions, looking at certain forms of queer kinship and how it's all so linked. The concerns are the same and it's funny to see the developments and the way that the freedom that queer writers have now is completely built on the shoulders of people who came before us. We're always writing in a continuum. I really appreciate that, it's been cool to realise. I went on a kind of spot-the-lesbians tour of Irish poetry, and I was reading them, one eye closed, kind of going, 'I think …' And then you find out anecdotally, *Oh yes, this person lived with their partner in a cottage for two thousand years*, and you're like, 'Right, okay!'

Mark: There's a thing in the States, they have a set of collectible trading cards of lesbian poets [from Headmistress Press]. I think we need our own thing here …

Sasha: I wanted to talk, Seán, a little bit about the project that we are going to be undertaking next year. It's very exciting: Seán is going to be appointed as the first ever poet in residence at the Irish Queer Archive in the National Library of Ireland, part of a Cúirt project. And then we'll be bringing the work that is written in response to that, delving through the archives, to Cúirt in 2022.

Seán: I'm so excited. I'm an academic in the daytime, so I spend a lot of time in archives, but I'm always looking at an old book or something, I'm never looking at this kind of living queer archive where there's so much that I'm excited to find out. And I think, like Liz said, that excavation work is really important in getting a sense of a community that's not just happened in a few years, or recently. I don't know what I'll find, but I've been looking through the catalogue and even the names of the items or the descriptions of what's in the box … I've already started a folder of like, 'Make sure to look at this', and 'This sounds like it could be a poem.'

Sasha: And given that you've said that you're comfortable putting anything on the page, I'm so keen to see what work is produced as a result.

Seán: Yeah. Well, I mean it's exciting as well because there's a lot about our 'I's and how those sit in the poem. And I'm looking forward to experimenting with other people's 'I's, and seeing through them and listening to them, what they have to say, and how do I make that into a poem? I'm really looking forward to the challenge.

Sasha: We have some questions now from the audience, so I'd like to put some to you. Fergus asks: *Which queer poets from the past do you admire? And how do you think that queer poetry or expression may have changed over time?* Liz, would you like to begin?

Liz: I mentioned Mary Dorcey. She would have been talismanic for me. At the moment, I'm very much 'living' with a second-wave feminist-activist poet called Minnie Bruce Pratt. I think she's in North Carolina and she writes an awful lot about how her queer life has intersected with legislation. When she realised she was a lesbian, she lost custody of her children under a statute called the Crime Against Nature Statute, so her actual existence made it so that she couldn't keep her children. Those kind of writers are for me right now. And they're still around, so the writers in the past are very much writers in the present as well.

Mark: Thom Gunn would definitely be a touchstone. I've been reading very slowly, purposely not letting myself read all of the collected poems. I'm reading the work slowly over two years because there is a finite amount of them. And I recently managed to snag from Books Upstairs a book from the 1980s called *The Penguin Book of Homosexual Verse*, which goes right back to the beginning of time, and right up to the 1970s. It's out of print, but it's basically our queer poetry history in one little book.

Seán: I have a copy of that too. There's a blurb on the back that says, 'This book proves the humanity of the homosexual', or something, a glowing review! For me, it would be Gerard Manley Hopkins. He's my favourite poet ever. I think it's interesting with someone like Gunn, when you see that confidence and explicitness building. It starts off really formal and then loosens, and there are things that the loose poems can say that the formal poems have to hide. And I think for Hopkins, what I like is that even though there's nothing – well, there are queer things in the poems, but it's the strangeness that is the obviously queer thing about Hopkins, and the way of looking at the world. And everything about subject matter, for Hopkins, doesn't matter. Well, I mean they are kind of sexual sometimes as well, but not on purpose, I think. But that strange way of looking at the world, having to contain the gaze somewhere else, the queer gaze focuses elsewhere, but you recognise it once you see it.

Sasha: We have a question from Fiachra: *What are some topics you would like to see explored in queer LGBTQ+ poetry and literature in the future, either by yourself or other poets?* Mark, do you want to kick us off this time?

Mark: The book that I'm working on is very much about house and home. That's a topic that I'm exploring at the moment, which is very different from the first collection. I think I would like it to be, I don't know, maybe a little bit lighter, a bit more humorous perhaps. Not funny poems, but to incorporate a bit more whimsy and musicality. Anything and everything – as long as it's a good poem, I don't really care, I'll read it.

Liz: For me, I just want to have poetry that's representative of a life lived on blast, and have everything be really fun and vibrant and sensual and alive and gutsy. I'm throwing down the gauntlet to myself, that the next thirty-six years are going to have a bit of craic in them, and I'll just see what I can knock out of those.

Seán: I think I would really like to see more trans voices and non-binary voices published, because with the exception of a few I know, there are really not enough. If I was excited to read any new queer poetry, I think that's what I would be most excited about.

Nessa O'Mahony

OLD WOES, NEW WAILS

Peggy O'Brien, *Tongues* (New Island Books, 2019), €14.95.
Greg Delanty, *No More Time* (Louisiana State University Press, 2020), $17.95.
Rowan Ricardo Phillips, *Living Weapon* (Faber & Faber 2021), £10.99.

Of all the tales of star-crossed lovers across the ages, that of twelfth-century lovers Héloïse and Abelard must rank among the most painful. Abelard, renowned scholar, falls for his young student, Héloïse, and is castrated by her family's connections as a result. Yet even mutilation can't keep the lovers apart; they vow to end their days cloistered together in a French monastery, kept apart by godly devotion. Their story gets a very modern upcycling, as well as a marked shift in tone, in Peggy O'Brien's retelling. *Tongues*, a verse narrative in six sections and fifty poems, is based loosely on a 1925 translation by CK Scott Moncrieff. In O'Brien's hands it becomes something deeper and more contemporary – an examination of power structures within human relationships.

The first half of the book is based on Abelard's extended letter, *Historia Calamitatum*; the second half is taken up with an epistolary exchange between him and Héloïse. In O'Brien's version, the calamity appears to be all of Abelard's own making – his sense of aggrieved self-worth propels him into confrontation after confrontation. The poetry is vivid and colloquial, and the narrative moves forward at a jaunty pace. In 'Ezekiel', the opening prose poem, we are told how Abelard 'got his mojo back, his / stature, even greater renown. Throughout Europe, he was / the man who could enumerate the infinite, then lost it all, / won and lost, again and again, his manhood, his way, his /wits, the plot'.

The tongue recurs as a motif, first appearing in 'Fosterling' as an image for the estuary Abelard tells us he was born on: 'I was born on an estuary, part river, part ocean, / A tongue speaking what's been to what will be', before he turns to the 'tidal dither' of the present. This Abelard is both man and literary product, and O'Brien's precise imagery captures that duality with great skill. 'I was fostered early, sent far away like a letter … // When I returned, I didn't speak to anyone, / Except the angel only I could see' ('Fosterling').

There are wonderfully detailed descriptions of the monastic life, where 'monks like brown wrens chirp their lauds and nones', but the key to successful verse narratives is credible characterisation and in this, O'Brien excels; she neatly captures the ambivalence of Abelard's character, his macho, egotistical cleverness combined with an outsider's vulnerability. His paramour, Héloïse, is equally credible, first adopting a more lyrical voice, reflecting in the poem 'Cincture' on how the woman must always pay higher costs for illicit love:

> The labour it takes to birth yourself from Hell,
> Sister, daughter, handmaiden, wife. You wear
> A chemise bound by a cincture to keep it together
> And bleat, 'When you left me, you took me with you.'

Before long, energetic exasperation reaches the surface: 'Who in God's name do you think you are? Abelard? / With your head so far up the arse of the Middle Ages' ('Virago'). This historic romance becomes a universal exploration of the many stages of love, from ecstasy to enervation and disillusionment. As the poem 'Midges' demonstrates – 'Yet again, crucifixion, resurrection. Tedious, / Rising and shining for yet another bash at it' – we resonate with lives where the only possible response is to acknowledge a universal *'mea maxima culpa'*.

Greg Delanty's latest collection, *No More Time*, is a compelling contribution to the debate about climate change. Its title suggests urgency, many of the poems combining elegy for that already lost to us, and celebration of that still managing to survive. In a prefatory note, Delanty describes an engraving on the floor of the American Museum of Natural History that states that the current rate of species loss is caused 'solely by humanity's transformation of the ecological landscape'. The poems reinforce that sense of humankind's culpability – the opening 'proem', titled 'Loosestrife', uses that pervasive, all-conquering weed as an analogy for the human species:

> Voices praise your magenta spread, your ability
> > to propagate by seed, by stem, by root,
> and how you adjust to light, to soil, spreading
> > your glory across the earth even as you kill
> by boat, by air, by land all before you

The spine of the collection is found in a 26-sonnet sequence, 'A Field Guide to People'. This offers an alphabetised encyclopaedia of species that are either thriving, on the cusp of extinction, or already extinct, and forms the opening and closing sections of the book. Beginning with 'Aye-Aye' (a breed of lemur) and concluding with 'Zanzibar Leopard', a breed that went extinct in the 1960s, each sonnet combines a Marianne Moore-like botanical precision with a Thunbergian preparedness to call it as it is. *'Bos taurus'*, for example, meditates on the toxic relationship between man and cow: 'What's tender? There's a deal on veal? Forget the poor / calf. Scruples flit like flies around the tail of a cow.'

Some images are so horrifying, they are indelible, as he says of the elephant in Dublin zoo that repetitively rocked because during its captivity in a circus van, rocking had been the only way that it could move ('Elephant'). More than once, prompted by the sense of outrage in an individual sonnet, this reader found herself googling the background of creatures mentioned, for example the Kāmaʻo, a species of Hawaiian thrush, once present in their millions and last heard singing in 1987, thus now presumed extinct. In Delanty's words, her 'song: a figment of my bird-brained imagination'.

‘A Field Guide to People’ is divided by a middle sequence, ‘Breaking News’, which contains 25 poems taking a broader view of the chaos we have brought upon ourselves. It opens with an untitled poem showing Gaia in a state of advanced dementia:

> Our slow realization redoubles despair.
> She doesn't recognize us. What hell
> she gives everyone, even those who care.
>
> Her aging body is becoming a living shell,
> *Terra Mater*, the erasing of cell after cell.

The poems in this section move from present to past, exploring the experiences of ‘conquistadors’ who have wreaked havoc on previous civilisations (‘While Reading the Diary of Christopher Columbus’), or presenting examples of human hubris that have led to destruction. In ‘The Great Ship’, the *Titanic* provides a neat metaphor for our current blind rush towards destruction:

> Crickets, cicadas, grasshoppers and frogs play on.
> What their song, their wing-music, is saying
>
> we can't say, except they must know already
> that the ice has gashed a gaping hole in the hull
>
> of Indian summer

Elsewhere, a jet's contrail is compared to a line of coke along a marble countertop. The topicality of a poem such as ‘Breaking News’ is made even stronger by the fact that as I read this poem, Texas was undergoing an unprecedented winter storm, whilst the Athenian Acropolis was blanketed in unseasonal drifts. As Delanty puts it: ‘It is below zero outside and we set fire / to our house in the middle of nowhere / to warm ourselves. Our very own pyre.’

One might argue that there isn't room for subtlety when the house is on fire, and a poem such as 'Any Way You Look at It', with its repetitions of 'No more time no more time', doesn't allow much space for interpretation. And yet, the final iteration of 'no more' might suggest a turning point in the collection, a recognition that nothing is yet inevitable. I don't want to over-state the collection's optimism – one of the final sonnet entries, 'X', evokes the recently lost Dingle emblem, Fungie the dolphin, after all. But with houses burning and ships sinking, it is good to be reminded that we can still, at least, sing in our rusting chains.

Living Weapon, American poet and essayist Rowan Ricardo Phillips's third collection, throbs with tension between the imagined and the real. It opens with a section from Wallace Stevens's extended poem 'Credences of Summer' and that poet's modernist preoccupation with the origins of art and imagination is visible throughout the volume. But in this case, the imagination is pitted against the twenty-first century world of political activism, and Phillips must explore how his 'unreal songs' can be sung 'in face / Of the object', as Stevens puts it.

The opening poem, an elegy for his grandmother ('Prelude'), sets a foreboding tone:

> My grandmother saw it coming and left.
> I'd already left. It came late and swift
> Like a tidal wave mistaken for a wave,
> Came, not as a note but as an octave

It also begins the argument about the usefulness of art in the face of calamity that sustains the collection: 'this elegy / Which, like all of them, is so useless and late'. So, '1776', the prose poem that follows as a meditation on one of New York's latest skyscrapers, is full of Wordsworthian and Yeatsian encounters with the numinous, yet even a glorious evocation of a murmuration of starlings or a description of the scraper's tower in this poem is questioned for its inherent worth: 'Things I tell myself to feel better about these pointless joyrides. / But in the end, that's all that they've been. Pointless joyrides. / I make nothing happen.'

Yeats's presence, explicit or implicit, is never far too far away. In 'The First Last Light in the Sky' we see 'The horizon, dragging its bulk, its lights / And salts, from under shifting sheets of sea', like some rough beast of Phillips's conjuring; it also emerges in the poem 'Violins', a meditation on art and violence:

> This is the brutal lesson of the twenty-first century,

Swilled like a sour stone
Through the vein of the beast

Who watches you while you eat

Not surprising in a book so intent on exploring the role of poetry in
a world gone mad, Phillips's poems are full of literary allusions, from
Heaney to Donne to Milton and Homer. Each reference sends the reader
back to the original poem, curious at how Phillips will recast it for his
own argument. 'Who is Less Than a Vapor?' takes Donne's 'Meditation
XII' at face value, echoing the Dean's opening line – 'What will not kill a
man if a vapour will? – almost exactly: 'What won't end a life if a vapor
will?' Elsewhere, the dialogue with a writer is more terse. In 'Tradition
and the Individual Talent', it is a two-line response to TS Eliot:

> I wandered through each chartered street
> Till I was shot by the police.

This reference to tradition reminds one that Phillips's frame of reference
in these poems is rarely American (despite the Wallace Stevens opening),
and whilst his political focus is domestic, the tradition to which he has
recourse is global. And for all his reservations about its limits, he, like all
poets, will always wait, as he says in 'The Question', for 'The part where
it all comes together, and, / Having come together, finally sings.'

Victoria Kennefick

IT DOESN'T MATTER WHAT YOU DO IT ONLY MATTERS THAT YOU DO IT

I am porous. Porous because air, liquid, harsh words, movie dialogue, a bloody sunset, the misaligned prongs of a fork, another person's mood pass through me, especially slowly. Porous as soil with good drainage. Porous as sound brick walls. Porous as paper, cardboard, sponges, pumice stones, untreated wood, and cork.

The term porosity comes, as words do, via circuitous routes, and is somewhere along that circumnavigation a derivative of Late Latin *porus* meaning 'a passage, a channel in the body'. *Porus* itself is a borrowing from the Greek *póros*, which is a 'means, a way out'. Both porosity and porous first appeared in a fourteenth-century English translation of a Latin encyclopedia of the sciences, an influential work that was written in the mid-thirteenth century. The reference was to the tongue, described as being 'porous and spongy'.

My first collection, *Eat or We Both Starve* (Carcanet Press, 2021), is replete with tongues, exploring as it does themes relating to appetite and consumption and the emergent guilt and shame we experience when we give ourselves over to these urges, or indeed when these natural desires are repressed. The speakers in the poems stick out their little tongues for Communion at mass (in medieval Christianity and Oriental art, large, protruding tongues are often the sign of demons or the devil), watch these cushioned masses loll on the delicious lips of partygoers, and one speaker even engages in a passionate French kiss with Audrey Hepburn, with 'seams popping'.

My constitution finds a soulmate in the tongue, sharing as we do permeability, yearnings to test and taste, and a reputation for sensitivity. On a practical level, it means I don't drink alcohol, for example. I can't. But even if *you* do enjoy a tipple, and (in the before time) I stood squashed up against you in a pub, or if we swayed near each other at a house party, or were seated next to each other at dinner, if I just briefly leaned in to listen to your best anecdote and your breath, golden-warm with whiskey tickled my nostrils, I'd become drunk too. On nothing but air. My boundaries dissolving like dry ice.

On the dance floor, in the theatre, at a poetry reading, watching a film, my skeleton wants to abandon me, leave me an absorbent heap on the floor, mopping up every snippet of conversation, loose change, and wad of discarded chewing gum. I want to wring out the whole world. I will admit that this can get embarrassing. But you don't need to know about that. I exhaust the fizzy-sherbet feeling so the next day, the next week I feel as if I have run out of joy. I go to work, and the mask is tight on my face. I want to scream in bathrooms, but everyone will hear me. How can I scream in the bathrooms without everyone hearing me?

Where to put all this? Where to wring it all out? What to *do*? I tried acting, I wasn't bad, but I had the taste of other peoples' words on my tongue. I painted a little, I wasn't bad, but the colours stained my fingers and when I gave my pictures away, I had no evidence they existed at all. When I was a child, until I was able to write, I shouted and shouted until nodules formed on my larynx. Then I yelled it out on the page. What else can I do with this? Tell me, what else can I do after I soak it all up? A pen and paper, a keyboard and screen with a flashing cursor – this is how I enact my existence. Writing and typing word after word, eking them out to keep them and to let them go like rivulets of black-on-white, making a channel for something to come through. A means. A passage. A way out. I am porous as paper, cardboard, sponges, pumice stones, untreated wood, and cork.

Notes on Contributors

Tamara Barnett-Herrin was born in London and currently lives in Los Angeles. She has written songs, poems, and sound-art installations for various performances and exhibitions. Her poem 'The Loves of The Plants' was published in *Fence*, Spring 2019.

Siobhán Campbell's latest collection is *Heat Signature* (Seren Books, 2017). Recent work exploring the intersections between human and non-human worlds appears in *Deep Time* (Black Bough Poetry), Poetry Archive's 'World View', and *Empty House* (Doire Press, 2021), edited by Alice Kinsella and Nessa O'Mahony.

As Co. na Mí é **Máirtín Coilféir**. Is léachtóir le Gaeilge é in Ollscoil Concordia, Montréal. Bailíodh dánta dá chuid sa chnuasach dátheangach *Calling Cards* (2019) agus foilsíodh leabhar critice leis, *Titley*, sa bhliain chéanna. Bhí sé seal ina eagarthóir liteartha ar an iris *Comhar*.

Philip Coleman teaches in the School of English, Trinity College Dublin, where he is also a Fellow. His edition of *The Selected Letters of John Berryman*, co-edited with Calista McRae, was published by Harvard University Press in 2020.

Sasha de Buyl is the Director of Cúirt International Festival of Literature, and a board member of GAZE, Dublin's International LGBTQ Film Festival.

Katie Donovan has published five collections of poetry with Bloodaxe Books. Her most recent, *Off Duty* (2016), was shortlisted for the *Irish Times* Poetry Now Award. She received the Lawrence O'Shaughnessy Award for Irish Poetry in 2017. She lives in Dalkey, Co. Dublin.

Jane Draycott's collections from Carcanet Press include *The Occupant* (a PBS Recommendation), *Over* (shortlisted for The TS Eliot Prize), and her 2011 translation of *Pearl*, the medieval dream-elegy. *Storms Under the Skin*, her translations from artist-poet Henri Michaux, is published by Two Rivers Press.

Ella Duffy's work has appeared in *The London Magazine*, *Ambit*, and *The Rialto,* among other outlets. She is the author of two poetry pamphlets, *Rootstalk* (Hazel Press) and *New Hunger* (Smith | Doorstop).

Sasha Dugdale's fifth collection, *Deformations* (Carcanet Press, 2020), was shortlisted for the TS Eliot Prize. She is a translator of Russian poetry and drama, including Maria Stepanova's collection *War of the Beasts and the Animals*, published this spring by Bloodaxe Books. From 2012 to 2017, she served as editor of *Modern Poetry in Translation*.

Nidhi Zak/Aria Eipe is a poet, pacifist, and fabulist. Born in India, she grew up across the Middle East, Europe, and North America, before calling Ireland home. Founder of the Play It Forward Fellowships, she is poetry editor at Skein Press and Fallow Media, and contributing editor with *The Stinging Fly*. Her debut poetry collection, *Auguries of a Minor God*, is forthcoming from Faber & Faber in July 2021.

Frank Farrelly is from Waterford. His poems are widely published. He won the Rush Poetry Prize, and was runner-up or shortlisted for a number of other competitions, including The Fish Poetry Prize, The Doolin Poetry Prize, Poets Meet Politics, North West Words, the Writing Spirit Award, and the Cúirt New Writing Prize.

Vona Groarke's eighth and experimental collection, *Link*, is forthcoming with The Gallery Press. Her last collection, *Double Negative* (2019), was shortlisted for the *Irish Times* Poetry Now Award. She lives in Co. Sligo and is currently working on a book of essay-readings of much-loved poems, *Up Close and Personal*.

Kerry Hardie's eighth collection, *Where Now Begins*, was published by Bloodaxe Books in 2020. Her previous book, *The Zebra Stood in the Night*, was shortlisted for the *Irish Times* Poetry Now Award. She has won many prizes both in Ireland and internationally, and her work is widely translated and anthologised.

Hugh Haughton is the author of *The Poetry of Derek Mahon* (Oxford University Press). He has edited *The Chatto Book of Nonsense Poetry* (Chatto & Windus, 1988), *Second World War Poems* (Faber & Faber, 2004), and (with Valerie Eliot) *The Letters of TS Eliot*, volumes 1 and 2. He teaches English at the University of York.

Seán Hewitt's debut collection, *Tongues of Fire* (Jonathan Cape, 2020), was shortlisted for the *Sunday Times* Young Writer of the Year Award, 2020. He is a poetry critic for *The Irish Times* and Teaching Fellow in Modern Literature at Trinity College Dublin.

Dane Holt's poems have been published in *Poetry Ireland Review*, *The Tangerine*, *The White Review*, and *The Honest Ulsterman*.

Kris Johnson was raised in Seattle, but is based in the UK. Her poetry has appeared in *Ambit, Poetry London, Poetry Northwest, The Rialto*, and *Hallelujah for 50ft Women* (Bloodaxe Books, 2015). She holds a Ph.D. in creative writing from Newcastle University.

Majella Kelly's debut pamphlet *Hush* was published by Ignition Press in 2020. Several of her poems around the theme of the Tuam Mother and Baby Home are published by Carcanet Press in the *Brotherton Poetry Prize Anthology*.

Victoria Kennefick's first poetry collection, *Eat or We Both Starve*, is published by Carcanet Press. Her work has appeared in *Poetry, The Poetry Review, PN Review, The Stinging Fly, Ambit*, and elsewhere. She is an Arts Council of Ireland Next Generation Artist.

Edward Larrissy's poems have appeared in *Sycamore Broadsheet 7*, the *Times Literary Supplement, Green River Review, Anglo-Welsh Review, The Observer, The Independent, The Faber Book of Science, Poetry Proper*, and in an e-pamphlet, *The Stories* (Argotist, 2012). He has edited T*he Cambridge Companion to British Poetry, 1945-2010*. From 2007 to 2013, he was Professor of Poetry at Queen's University, Belfast.

Bryony Littlefair is a poet, community worker, and workshop facilitator, living in London. Her pamphlet *Giraffe* won the Mslexia Pamphlet Competition in 2017, and her first collection, *Escape Room*, will be published by Seren Books in 2022.

Michael Longley has received many awards, among them the TS Eliot Prize and The Queen's Gold Medal for Poetry. In 2015 he was made a Freeman of the City of Belfast, where he and his wife, the critic Edna Longley, live and work. His twelfth collection, *The Candlelight Master*, was published by Jonathan Cape in 2020.

Seán Lysaght is the author of six volumes of poems, including *Scarecrow* (1998), *The Mouth of a River* (2007), and *Carnival Masks* (2014), all from The Gallery Press. He has also written prose about wildlife and landscapes: *Eagle Country* (2018) and *Wild Nephin* (2020). His *Selected Poems* appeared from The Gallery Press in 2010. He lives in Westport, Co. Mayo.

John McAuliffe's fifth book is *The Kabul Olympics* (The Gallery Press, 2020). His *Selected Poems* will be published later this year.

Mícheál McCann is from Derry. His poems have appeared recently in *The Manchester Review, Ambit, fourteen poems*, and *Banshee Lit*. His first pamphlet, *Safe Home*, was published by Green Bottle Press in 2020. He lives in Belfast.

Thomas McCarthy was born Co. Waterford and educated at UCC. He worked for many years at Cork City Libraries. His collections of poetry include *Pandemonium* and *Prophecy*, both from Carcanet Press. He has won the Patrick Kavanagh Award as well as the Ireland Funds Annual Literary Award. He is a former editor of *Poetry Ireland Review*, and a member of Aosdána.

Tim McGabhann's first two novels, *Call Him Mine* and *How to Be Nowhere*, are published by Weidenfeld and Nicolson. His fiction, non-fiction, and poetry have also appeared in *The Stinging Fly*, the *Dublin Review*, *gorse*, *The Tangerine*, and *Winter Papers*.

David McLoghlin is the author of *Waiting for Saint Brendan and Other Poems* (2012), *Santiago Sketches* (2017), and *Crash Centre* (forthcoming, 2021), all with Salmon Poetry. He recently returned to live in Ireland after ten years in New York City.

Emily Middleton lives in London and works in digital government. She is a former winner of the Foyle Young Poets of the Year Award and the Tower Poetry Competition. Her poems are published in *The Rialto*, *Mslexia*, and *Acumen*.

Audrey Molloy is the author of the chapbook *Satyress* (Southword Editions, 2020). Her first full collection, *The Important Things*, is published by The Gallery Press later this year. In 2019 she received the Hennessy Award for Emerging Poetry. She is currently pursuing a master's degree in Creative Writing at Manchester Metropolitan University.

File agus drámadóir í **Ceaití Ní Bheildiúin**. Bhuaigh an cnuasach filíochta is déanaí uaithi, *Agallamh sa Cheo – Cnoc Bhréanainn, 52.2352°T, 10.2544°I*, Duais an Oireachtais, 2018. Bronnadh sparánachtaí Ealaín na Gaeltachta uirthi, 2019 agus 2020.

Niamh NicGhabhann is an art historian and senior lecturer in the Department of History, University of Limerick. Her research explores Irish art and architecture. Her book, *Medieval Ecclesiastical Buildings in Ireland, 1789-1915: Building on the Past* was published by Four Courts Press in 2015, and she is currently working on a book on Catholic architecture in Ireland between 1829 and 1936.

File agus scríbhneoir do pháistí í **Áine Ní Ghlinn**. 31 leabhar foilsithe aici agus gradaim éagsúla bronnta ar a saothar filíochta agus próis. Í ina Laureate na nÓg 2020-2023. Tá sí ag obair faoi láthair ar úrscéal nua do dhéagóirí agus ar chnuasach nua filíochta.

Is tobar gan bhonn é aoibhneas Chorca Dhuibhne, a thugann ardú meoin do **Bhríd Ní Mhóráin** agus inspioráid leanúnach dá saothar. Thaitin a tréimhse mar scríbhneoir cónaitheach ag Oidhreacht Chorca Dhuibhne le hurraíocht ó Ealaín na Gaeltachta (2003-2018) thar barr léi. Tá seacht gcnuasach foilsithe aici.

Bernard O'Donoghue was born in Cullen, Co. Cork. His most recent book of poems is *The Seasons of Cullen Church* (Faber & Faber, 2016).

Proinsias Ó Drisceoil is the author of many essays on the Gaelic literature and literary history of Scotland and Ireland. His publications include *Ar Scaradh Gabhail: An Fhéiniúlacht in Cín Lae Amhlaoibh Uí Shúilleabháin* (2000), and *Seán Ó Dálaigh: Éigse agus Iomarbhá* (2007). He edited *Culture in Ireland : Regions, Identity and Power* (1993).

Tá trí leabhar filíochta foilsithe ag **Simon Ó Faoláin** agus dhá leabhar d'aistriúcháin liteartha. I measc na ngradam atá buaite ag a chuid scríbhneoireachta tá Duais Glen Dimplex, Duais Strong, Duais Bhaitéar Uí Mhaicín, Duais Cholm Cille agus Duais Foras na Gaeilge. Tá sé ina stiúrthóir ar An Fhéile Bheag Filíochta agus ina bhunaitheoir agus eagarthóir ar an iris liteartha Gaeilge *Aneas*.

Nessa O'Mahony, a Dublin-born poet, has published five books of poetry: *Bar Talk* (1999), *Trapping a Ghost* (2005), *In Sight of Home* (2009), *Her Father's Daughter* (2014), and *The Hollow Woman on the Island* (Salmon Poetry, 2019).

Dhá chnuasach filíochta le **Seosamh Ó Murchú** atá foilsithe, *Taisí Tosta* (2015) agus *Athchuairt* (2019). Tá sé ina Eagarthóir Sinsearach sa Ghúm agus bhí sé ina chomheagarthóir ar an iris liteartha *Oghma* (1989-99). Is as Loch Garman ó dhúchas dó agus tá cónaí air le fada i mBaile Átha Cliath.

Liz Quirke's debut collection, *The Road, Slowly*, was published by Salmon Poetry in 2018. She is completing a Ph.D. in Poetry by Creative Practice at NUI Galway, on Queer Kinship in Contemporary Poetry. She teaches poetry at NUI Galway, and divides her time between Galway and Kerry.

Kimberly Reyes is the author of *Running to Stand Still* (Omnidawn, 2019), *Warning Coloration* (dancing girl press, 2018), and *Life During Wartime* (Fourteen Hills, 2019). Published and anthologised in numerous international outlets, Kimberly was a 2019-2020 Fulbright Fellow at University College Cork.

Aoife Riach's poetry has been published in *Crannóg, Sonder, Channel, Abridged, The Pickled Body, The Kilkenny Poetry Broadsheet*, and other magazines. She was a 2019 Irish Writers' Centre Young Writer Delegate and was shortlisted for the Marian Keyes Young Writer Award.

Maurice Riordan was born in Lisgoold, Co. Cork. He edited The *Finest Music: Early Irish Lyrics* (Faber & Faber, 2014) and is a former editor of *The Poetry Review*. His fifth collection from Faber, *The Shoulder Tap,* will be published in 2021. He lives in London.

Declan Ryan has published two pamphlets, the first in the *Faber New Poets* series (2014), and *Fighters, Losers* (New Walk Editions, 2019). His reviews and essays have appeared in *The New York Review of Books*, the *Times Literary Supplement*, the *Los Angeles Review of Books, Poetry*, and elsewhere.

Stephen Sexton's first book, *If All the World and Love Were Young* (Penguin Books, 2019), was the winner of the Forward Prize for Best First Collection and the Shine / Strong Award for Best First Collection. In 2020 he was awarded the EM Forster Award from the American Academy of Arts and Letters, and The Rooney Prize for Irish Literature.

Damian Smyth has published six collections since 2000, the latest being *English Street* (Templar Poetry) in 2018. *Irish Street* is due in 2021.

Maria Stepanova is a Russian poet, novelist, essayist, journalist, and the author of ten poetry collections and three books of essays. Her book *War of the Beasts and the Animals*, translated by Sasha Dugdale (in which the full sequence 'The Body Returns' appears), is the first English translation of her poetry. It is published by Bloodaxe Books, and is a PBS Translation Choice. 'The Body Returns' was originally commissioned by Hay International Festival to commemorate the centenary of the First World War.

Jess Thayil's poems have appeared in *The Stinging Fly, The Tangerine, Poetry NI, The Seventh Quarry, Black Bough Poetry, Magma Poetry, Ink Sweat & Tears, Abstract Magazine TV, Whale Road Review*, and *Potomac Review*. She's also a self-taught artist specialising in abstract paintings.

Mark Ward is the author of the chapbooks *Circumference* (Finishing Line Press, 2018) and *Carcass* (Seven Kitchens Press, 2020), and the full-length collection *Nightlight* (Salmon Poetry, 2022). He is the founding editor of *Impossible Archetype*, an international journal of LGBTQ+ poetry.

Grace Wilentz is a poet based in Dublin's The Liberties. Her first collection, *The Limit of Light* (The Gallery Press), was named one of the best books of 2020 in the *Irish Examiner*. She is a recent recipient of a literature bursary from The Arts Council / An Chomhairle Ealaíon.